D1716684

Old
Collections
New
Audiences

Decorative Arts
and Visitor Experience
for the 21st Century

Henry Ford Museum & Greenfield Village provides unique educational experiences based on authentic objects, stories and lives from America's traditions of ingenuity, resourcefulness and innovation. Our purpose is to inspire people to learn from these traditions to help shape a better future.

Henry Ford Museum & Greenfield Village is an independent, nonprofit educational organization, not affiliated with Ford Motor Company or the Ford Foundation.

Editors
Donna R. Braden and Gretchen W. Overhiser

Copy Editor
Susan M. Steele

Publications Assistant
Tina Glengary

Photo Credits
Page 9 – Courtesy of Winterthur Museum
Page 19 – Program Brochure, Courtesy The Bard Graduate Center for Studies in the Decorative Arts
Page 38 – Courtesy the Victoria and Albert Musem
Page 50 – Furniture Exhibit, Courtesy Henry Ford Museum & Greenfield Village
Page 56 – Baltimore Painted Furniture Exhibition, Phase II. Photograph by David Prencipe.
          Courtesy The Maryland Historical Society
Page 64 – At Home with Baltimore Painted Furniture, Phase II. Photograph by David Prencipe.
          Courtesy The Maryland Historical Society
Page 74 – Spencer-Peirce-Little House, Newbury, Massachusetts. Photograph by J. David Bohl.
          Courtesy the Society for the Preservation of New England Antiquities
Page 76 – Living Room Vignette. Courtesy the Society for the Preservation of New England Antiquities
Page 80 – View of the label rail in the Billiard Room. Courtesy The Newark Museum
Page 89 – Storybook illustration for the Parlor. Courtesy The Newark Museum

Design
JEROME, New York

Printing
University Lithoprinters, Inc.
Ann Arbor, Michigan

ISBN 0-933728-04-2

Henry Ford Museum & Greenfield Village
20900 Oakwood Boulevard
Dearborn, Michigan 48124
(313) 271-1600
www.hfmgv.org

Furniture cartoon graphic (on cover) by John Moga.

This publication was made possible by a generous grant from The Americana Foundation.

Old Collections

New Audiences

Decorative Arts
and Visitor Experience
for the 21st Century

Table of Contents

TRANSFORMING EXPERIENCES THROUGH VISITOR STUDIES

A FRESH LOOK AT HISTORIC HOUSES

ENTERING THE 21st CENTURY: Responses to the Essays

Preface

These papers were presented at Henry Ford Museum, in Dearborn, Michigan, in November 1999, as part of a national symposium entitled *Old Collections, New Audiences: Decorative Arts and Visitor Experience for the 21st Century*. The goals of the symposium were:

- to bring together in a unique way a wide range of people from institutions that address issues of learning and visitor experience in the decorative arts, such as art museums, history museums, historic houses and decorative arts institutions, as well as academic fields of study;
- to involve a national body of speakers and participants;
- to focus on how learning theories have been applied to practice in the decorative arts. Although theories might originate from different places (e.g., visitor studies, art education), it was their practical application that was of interest to us; and
- to ensure that attendees left with knowledge of the best practices in the field.

This symposium was actually the culmination of a several-year effort at Henry Ford Museum & Greenfield Village to learn about and experiment with ways to make its decorative arts collections more relevant to modern visitors. The major component of this effort was a series of upgrades to the Museum's furniture exhibit (completed in 1998 and described in the essays by Nancy Bryk and by Donna Braden and Gretchen Overhiser).

To our knowledge, this was the first national symposium in which decorative arts and visitor experience were looked at together. We had found repeatedly in our readings, museum visits and conversations with other museum people that, for the most part, decorative arts and visitor experience lived in two very different worlds. Decorative arts studies were about connoisseurship, maker histories and style features. In contrast, developing and understanding visitor experiences involved things like visitor studies, educational programs and design philosophies. We thought that it was long past time for these two camps to meet together and forge a new relationship into the future. The enthusiastic speakers and audience who attended the November symposium thought so, and we hope that you will too!

Donna R. Braden, Henry Ford Museum & Greenfield Village

The Question of Decorative Arts

Nancy Bryk, Curator
Henry Ford Museum & Greenfield Village

It seems to me that the "decorative arts" have always been betwixt and between in the museum world. They are not really considered "fine art"—art created for art's sake out of the heart and soul of the artist to inspire and move. Nor are they steam engines or other workhorses produced only to be useful. The decorative arts are as useful as they are beautiful. On occasion we've just put them out in galleries along with fine art and expect that our visitors will appreciate their sculptural beauty. But listening to visitors and watching their reactions to these furnishings is fascinating. Yes, they do marvel at the beauty of such pieces. But many are naturally curious about the "people issues" connected to these wonderful furnishings. Questions they ask might include: Did someone famous use this? Why does it look this way? Were the owners rich? What's it like to sit on this? What type of old-fashioned house did it sit within?

We've learned at Henry Ford Museum that addressing both issues of design and the practical issues of furniture use arrests our visitors' attention. We converse with visitors about why the piece looks the way that it does from an aesthetic angle as well as a human-need angle. In fact, I might suggest, as others have, that we re-name these collections "household furnishings." This term will remind us that these objects were designed by, made and used for people within the home. The term may help to remind us to keep people issues in our conversations about these pieces. Furthermore, it's a lot less off-putting than the term "decorative arts."

In fact, within the last three years, Henry Ford Museum & Greenfield Village has moved the decorative arts away from a discussion of style and period to conversations that address the household furnishings angle and focus on the user and the maker. We've discovered, through various furniture exhibits that we deemed failures, that beautiful and "important" objects don't always stand on their own and galvanize our visitors. We now know that presentation—including tone, visitor interaction, labeling, object choice and setting—has everything to do with whether the household furnishings are interesting and relevant to our visitors. But this has not always been the case.

Twenty years ago, as a young intern here at Henry Ford Museum, I walked the long halls displayed with our marvelous furniture collections. The period rooms we had were designer-perfect, but rather sterile and without human context. Labeling was at a bare minimum. Our curators, who were the only ones who decided what was displayed, chose our higher-style masterpieces of furniture for exhibit. We never questioned their choices or the importance of the pieces.

But our visitors did not come to see the furniture. Nor did they stay long when they meandered unwittingly into the area. I was curious as to why these galleries were not popular. The objects were lovely. And they were furnishings—couldn't *everyone* relate to them?

It seemed that our new president of the organization certainly couldn't relate to the furniture either. The curators had not convinced him with their exhibition that the furniture was an important part of the American story of industrialization or domestic life. So, these furniture galleries were extensively dismantled in the early 1980s. Several pieces were sent to a small, retro-filled exhibit space within the Museum's Great Hall, but most were relegated to storage.

The curatorial staff bolstered itself for calls and complaints from the public. To their dismay, just a handful complained. That lack of response from our visitors regarding the loss of most of the furniture on exhibit was an eye-opening experience for a fledgling curator like me. A question many asked, including myself, was: If the collection is unpopular and largely in storage, why bother to have it at all? Who was going to see these pieces again? Should we keep them out of view from scholars and visitors by closing them up in storage? If they're unpopular, the chance of getting much back on the Museum floor was remote.

An institutional dictum is that it is part of our job to deploy objects within programs and exhibits that effectively help us get our mission across. If our furniture couldn't do that, we had a problem. What might be the fate of this collection if it could not speak to our visitors or to our mission? Of course, the curators instinctively knew the collections *could* be made interesting and could tell a mission-related story. It was our job to make them interesting. But how could we do this?

The happy ending is that The Americana Foundation challenged us to reinvigorate our rather moribund display and put furniture—and its makers and users—squarely within the hearts and minds of our visitors. In the late 1990s, no longer a young intern, I was part of a team of curators and exhibit developers who rose to the challenge of making the furniture a "must-see" exhibit. We understood that it was not the furniture's fault that it was largely shunned by our visitors, but its environment, the choices of objects, the labels and the level of knowledge visitors were expected to bring to the exhibit. Give us a chance, we thought, and we can make a great exhibit! So we rolled up our sleeves and went to work.

In a process that will be fleshed out further in this publication by Donna Braden and Gretchen Overhiser, curators and project staff put aside all presumptions of what an exhibit of furniture should look like. We searched for ways of connecting modern visitors with these collections by approaching these objects with visitors' eyes. How did we do this? Many different ways, including asking visitors to look at and respond to photos of furnishings in our collections. Which did they like best? What questions did they trigger?

Second, the curators decided to put aside thoughts of connoisseurship for awhile and ask a different set of questions—questions our visitors might ask. We tried to "mind-meld" with our visitors' natural curiosity and see what each piece of furniture said to them. We asked questions about the makers and users, including: Why does it look this way? Who made it? What tells us he was an expert? How is this design peculiar to *this* maker? Do we think the design was "successful" (that is, was its function clear, was it sturdy and did we find it aesthetically pleasing)? Did *contemporaneous* folks find it successful? Avant-garde? Is this design peculiar or typical? Where was the piece used within a house? Did it have cultural meaning we needed to explain? Was it integral to a specific social ritual? Did it have an interesting story associated with it that wasn't obvious by just looking at it? We jumped into learning about cultural contexts, habits, expectations of a well-furnished house, relative expense and industrialization of the industry in ways that we hadn't before.

Donna and Gretchen asked us to think about delivery method. Keep labels short. Don't tell visitors everything we know about a piece—yawn—let them discover things on their own. Can we let visitors manipulate things on their own? Sit in reproduction chairs? How can we bring visitors into the subject rather than keeping them at arm's length?

These issues and questions have become fairly standard now that we are examining the rest of our household furnishings collections, particularly questions involving social ritual. We've come a long way from simply putting lovely things against marble walls. We now try to understand what objects and subjects pique our visitors' curiosity. The "school of hard knocks" helped us discover that collections should reflect some of the experiences (and furnishings) of newer generations. A variety of staff with varying viewpoints together create exhibits that offer our visitors varied ways of learning about this message. Perhaps hardest of all, we have to restrain ourselves from relentlessly offering important information or our own learned opinions—maybe we should let our visitors discover some things on their own.

The result of this team-based process of inquiry and exhibit development is that we crafted an exhibit that we think is fundamentally different than the period rooms were 15 years ago. We were willing to take chances. We put in sit-upon-able chairs, anthropomorphized chairs in cartoon labels, included abbreviated labels and created a small room-setting in which a battle over furniture is afoot accompanied by comic audio tapes—all this about furniture! Our visitors seem to think the furniture is fun and interesting to look at. The curators are delighted to see visitors take renewed interest in a collection previously regarded as boring. And we hope that people are learning something about these household furnishings.

We still remind ourselves that it is acceptable to break conventional rules of exhibits. What do we have to lose? After all, risk-takers are rewarded, aren't they? The old ways haven't worked particularly well. We hope that you'll embrace the ideas and experiences of other institutions presented within these pages with an open mind and a sense of adventure. What do *you* have to lose? Your collection, your institution and your visitors have much to gain. If an unusual approach isn't successful, you've still learned something. The school of hard knocks has taught us much. We're happy to share our experiences with you.

Our Collective Challenge:
Fostering Visual Literacy in the 21st Century

Dorothy Dunn, Head of Education
Cooper-Hewitt, National Design Museum, Smithsonian Institution

The Symposium *Old Collections, New Audiences: Decorative Arts and Visitor Experience for the 21st Century* brought together a remarkable group of educators and curators to consider how to make decorative arts collections in museums and historic homes relevant to our audiences today and in the future. I applaud the education and curatorial staff at Henry Ford Museum & Greenfield Village who worked very hard to organize this conference—Donna Braden, Gretchen Overhiser, Jeanine Head Miller, Hank Prebys, Nancy Bryk and Heather Seeley—and The Americana Foundation, for its generous sponsorship.

This conference generated an atmosphere of mutual support between museum educators and curators, making old news of the adversarial relationship between these two areas of expertise within the world of museums. Museums are defined by their collections and by their audiences and we need to recognize the symbiotic relationship between curators and educators. Simply put, we need each other. Only by respecting the insights and expertise that we both bring to our institutions can we offer the exhibitions and programs that will attract and be meaningful to audiences, allowing us to be valid and vital institutions in the 21st century.

Many museums and historic homes have conducted visitor studies, and several conference presentations shared visitor research methods including gallery observation, focus groups, surveys and studies of human development and diverse learning styles. Such work has had a huge impact on the development of exhibitions, labels, interpretive and interactive strategies, and educational programs that have made museums more inclusive as they have become more engaging, relevant and entertaining. We can all learn a great deal from visitor studies conducted by other institutions, and it is important that we maintain a network of conferences, publications, meetings, etc., to share such work. It is also clear, however, that the experience of conducting visitor research for one's own institution results in true believers. Institutions that have engaged in visitor research have shaped the study around their own unique circumstances. Such studies also offer opportunities for curators and educators to work and to learn together. The mutual support and respect shared by professional teams from museums who had conducted visitor research were impressive.

This conference was particularly timely for Cooper-Hewitt, National Design Museum, Smithsonian Institution, as we are currently planning galleries that will feature the Museum's permanent collections, to open in 2002. As most of you know, the Museum is housed in the historic Carnegie Mansion on 91st Street and Fifth Avenue in New York City. Cooper-Hewitt, National Design Museum is the only museum in the United States that is dedicated to exploring the creation and consequences of the designed environment: the objects we use, the spaces in which we live and work, and our visual forms of communication. At the National Design Museum, decorative arts collections are presented in the broad context of design.

For the past ten years, under the inspired leadership of Dianne H. Pilgrim, Director, the National Design Museum has developed a variety of educational programs for school and educator audiences. The Museum's exhibitions and collections provide ideas and inspiration for these programs. The collections are also studied to learn how humans throughout history have shaped the world around them to meet their most basic as well as their most extraordinary needs. The Museum's programs reference our audience's experiences every day and invite them to gain new awareness about how their lives are shaped by design.

Exhibition *Activity Guides* engage young visitors in the design process while they tour Museum exhibitions with professional museum teachers. These guides feature activities that encourage young visitors to look closely, to articulate their observations through discussion and sketching, to think like designers, and to share their design ideas through sketching and model building. The guides, developed to help students bridge their Museum visit and their daily life experiences, are designed to stand on their own and are distributed as educational resources beyond the exhibition dates.

As an example of activities included in the guides, "Design Journal" (published in 1991) featured two seemingly similar, yet vastly different activities inspired by the Museum's collection of historic and contemporary place settings. One activity provided a circle, representing a dinner plate, and asked young visitors to decorate the plate based on a decoration they found in the galleries. In such an activity, sketching becomes a method to foster close observation. The next activity, entitled "Design a Feast," engaged students in design. No circle representing a plate was offered for this exercise. This activity was introduced by the parameters of the design challenge: students first filled out a menu and an invitation card for a feast. This information established the parameters of their design challenge. A feast of nuts, grubs and berries for bears calls for a very different design solution than an 18-course meal in a palace or a picnic on the moon. Designers always work within parameters shaped by the user, place, time, materials, budget, etc. Students rose to the challenge and designed very innovative and creative solutions for one of the most basic human needs: eating. For instance, one student decided that his feast was a picnic and he used a frisbee for the plate. After using it to eat his meal, he would use it to play. This represents design thinking.

Many of the activities and strategies that we develop for the galleries become the focus for the Museum's programs for educators. We recognize K-12 educators as our best partners in exploring the potential for design education to enrich the school curriculum and to help relate the curriculum to the real world. In addition to the resources featured in Museum exhibitions, we often tap the Museum's strong relationship to the design community—architects and graphic, environmental, media, fashion and product designers—as an important resource in programs for educators. Exhibition-related workshops for educators as well as the annual *Summer Design Institute* and *City of Neighborhoods: Bridging School and Community* are opportunities for K-12 educators and designers to work together. The design studio provides the model for all of our programs. Our primary goal is to engage educators, in their own right, in the design process and to enjoy the pleasure and power of making things that work. We then reflect on these experiences to synthesize how the design studio experience and the design process can enhance teaching and learning in the K-12 classroom.

Design Directions is a comprehensive design awareness and design education program for high school students. Like our programs for educators, *Design Directions* offers students opportunities to work directly with professional designers through workshops, studio visits, internships and portfolio workshops. This program encourages urban youth to enter design programs at colleges and universities and, ultimately, to enter and diversify design professions.

While the National Design Museum is in a unique position to present objects in the context of design, the Museum's home, the historic Andrew Carnegie mansion, suggests what I think is our collective challenge to make authentic objects relevant to 21st century audiences. Andrew Carnegie supported the building of public libraries across the United States and Great Britain. When Andrew Carnegie was a poor factory boy living in Pittsburgh, he was given access to a wealthy man's private library because he showed promise. Carnegie identified this access as key to his ability to improve himself and his situation, resulting in his success. As a philanthropist, he donated enormous amounts of money to fund public libraries during the 19th and early 20th centuries. He contributed to our country's commitment to providing public education and institutions that promote literacy. By literate, I mean the ability to walk into a public library with confidence (a sense of belonging), to find a book or a periodical that is relevant to one's interest, pull it from the shelf or stacks, read it, and be improved through this access to information. This definition of literacy also suggests that, as a citizen, I am able to use the power of words and language to write a letter, a brief, a book, a sign, etc., in order to communicate my ideas and to improve the world.

What would happen if you took an informal survey of members of your community and asked them this question: If your community can only afford to support a public library or a public museum, which would you support? Without doubt, the majority of your interviewees would answer, "the library." The library represents our right as citizens to be literate and no one questions its importance. However, many of the people you interview would describe themselves as "visual" people. And no one would question that we live in a visual world. Where in our educational systems, however, do we prepare citizens to be visually literate? Where and when do we learn the skills that we need to look closely and carefully at the world around us, to articulate what we see and draw meaningful conclusions based on our observations? When and where do we learn the methods and processes to shape the world around us and to communicate ideas visually to make the world better? In a visual world, the skills inherent in visual literacy should have equal importance with those skills relevant to verbal literacy.

Our collective challenge is to place museums on par with libraries within our communities and to offer schools and the general public opportunities to exercise the skills relevant to visual literacy. Libraries have books. Museums have objects. Like books, objects provide insights into the world and its social, cultural and environmental issues—past, present and future. Museum professionals have access to the invaluable insights represented by the objects in our collections. It is exciting to consider the possibilities and opportunities for making such insights more accessible and meaningful for our audiences in years to come.

Listening to Our Visitors' Voices

Beth A. Twiss-Garrity, Curator of Education
Winterthur Museum, Garden and Library

If "old collections" are to attract, interest and inspire "new audiences," museum professionals in decorative arts museums must listen to what visitors say about themselves and museum collections. What are visitor motivations for and desires in learning about decorative arts? Are they the same as those of museum professionals? And once having listened, museum staffs need to use this information in exhibition and program planning in substantive and meaningful ways.

This paper will outline how one decorative arts museum developed research strategies for uncovering the motivations, expectations and thinking strategies of its visitors. First, research techniques will be described, then conclusions will be explained, and finally a couple of the ways in which these theories have been put into practice will be reviewed. The goal is to give some answers to: *Why* do decorative arts museums need to listen to their visitors? *How* do they listen? And *what* can be learned?

Winterthur, the museum in question, has a large collection of decorative arts used or made in America between 1640 and 1860. For the last ten years, visitor research has been done within the Education, Public Programs and Visitor Service Division by the Education Research Team (hereafter referred to as

ERT).[1] The individuals who form the group are charged in their job descriptions with implementing interpretive strategies for that collection for audiences ranging from preschool through senior citizen.

Following a grant from the National Endowment for the Humanities to write a *Handbook for Interpreters* in the late 1980s,[2] the ERT began to consider what might be a relevant interpretation of all this "old stuff" for the increasing variety of audiences coming at that point in time and those that might be attracted in the future. The ERT concluded that its professional interest and passion for the decorative arts alone were not sufficient. Reading in the fields of museum education and visitor studies convinced team members that they needed to learn more about visitors first-hand.

In conducting its studies, the ERT developed four working tenets for doing qualitative visitor research. First, the team developed and implemented the studies themselves. At the time of the first study, the members of the group had neither formal training in visitor research nor the resources to hire consultants. However, they felt empowered by work at the Denver Art Museum and the Getty to undertake simple exploratory studies[3] that forced team members to talk to and listen to visitors. Because team members did the work, a high level of excitement and commitment to using what was learned resulted in the lessons being incorporated into future planning. The primary methods used were informal focus groups and one-on-one interviews using open-ended questions.

A second important factor was the method for analyzing the answers to open-ended questions. The ERT adopted a sociological research framework called grounded theory.[4] Grounded theory helps researchers discover theory that explains or predicts behavior rather than simply verifying existing theory. Research projects began with a hypothesis born of reading in the field, leading to a question or series of questions to ask visitors. Questions were tested with a small group of visitors first to see if they led to helpful responses. Then, as answers were gathered from visitors, patterns in the data were searched for, leading to adoption of the hypothesis or its refinement into new theory.

Thirdly, the ERT read widely. The group began with the questions that many other museum professionals ask: Why do visitors come? What do visitors learn? How can I help them to "read an object?"[5] The literature review expanded, however, into a variety of fields, chosen sometimes by the content of visitors' answers and sometimes by serendipitous discoveries. The visitor research in this paper was informed by theories on the act of reading from the formal education world, cognitive neuroscience, leisure studies and economic models for consumer behavior.

Finally, the ERT has always thought of its research as organic and ongoing, just like the visitors' experiences observed. Future studies with new audiences may lead to refinements or whole new theories.

Current emerging theories from visitor research to date can be organized in the following ways. What draws people to Winterthur, or decorative arts museums? Once there, how do visitors think about the collections, and what sorts of experiences are they seeking?

What draws people to an exhibition is often referred to in visitor studies literature as "the grab," something about the collection or object that attracts visitors to want to attend to it.[6] What is the "grab" of a decorative arts museum? Is it wanting to learn something, for example, about ball and claw feet? Is it a pretty, quiet place to spend time with friends? Often researchers have framed these questions as a dichotomy of education versus recreation.[7]

The ERT found in listening to Winterthur's visitors that they often could not make such a distinction.[8] Not only was education versus recreation a false dichotomy but Museum staff members also learned that they had misunderstood the nuances of what visitors have been saying. Visitors sometimes defined words differently than staff did.

In a series of focus groups studying motivation to attend a decorative arts museum, visitors articulated seven attractive attributes for a visit:

- a desire for amusement;
- to be engulfed in history;
- to receive an education;
- as a place for recreation;
- as a place for learning;
- to be inspired by beauty;
- and, to have a social experience.

A single visitor's motivation might have been a mixture of the list. Note also that these were the motivations visitors articulated to researchers. For example, since only one visitor in the focus groups came to the Museum alone, the social nature of the experience probably was important for almost all the visitors, although only seven percent claimed it outright.

Four of the attributes—education, learning, recreation and entertainment—seem to get to the heart of the question about the role of a museum. Is it for education, entertainment, or even edutainment? In Figure 1, the segments representing percentages of visitors who described their motivation to visit a museum to be for amusement and education are small, while the segments for recreation and learning are large. The ERT decided to explore further what visitors meant by these words.

Amusement as defined by visitors, and by *Webster's*,[9] is entertainment. It is receiving a pleasurable diversion; it is a passive experience that happens to people

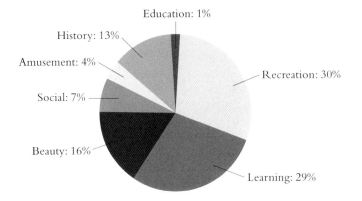

**FIGURE 1: Visitor Motivations (Winterthur focus groups 1998)
ERT Focus Group Measures**

while they watch or listen. Education likewise is a more passive experience, whereby people receive formal instruction. As one of the visitors said about his visit to Winterthur, "Well, part was fun, but part was education too. And education is probably a bad word. I think about all the things I missed in school because I really didn't care at that time." While amusement or education are not inherently bad—some visitors value them and they have their place—most visitors do not look for them in a museum.

Visitors, on the other hand, articulated recreation and learning much more often as motivating factors for a visit. Recreation, though it is often thought of in popular literature as a leisure activity involving a sport, is by definition any activity that restores or refreshes. When visitors were asked to describe what a recreational activity was for them and then to describe what prompted a visit to our museum, their answers resembled each other. They saw the museum as a place to escape from everyday life, a physical retreat from material tasks, one that could restore and refresh.

The way in which visitors described "learning" as distinct from education was perhaps one of the most enlightening parts of the research. While museum literature tends to use the two words interchangeably, visitors used "learning" in a distinct way that matches its true meaning. In *learning*, visitors gain an understanding through self-discovery, whereas in *education*, visitors are instructed in skills and information. "I always like to go someplace I've never been before, learn new things and expand horizons. See things I've never seen before."

Note the use of the word "see." One of the most frustrating parts of the ERT's early forays into visitor research was the large number of visitors who would respond that they came to Winterthur "to see everything," because they were "sight-seeing" or they just wanted "to see what was here." Winterthur was a notch on their tourist belt; once they had seen it, they could move on to someplace else.

Focus group scripts were drafted twice in order to find ways to probe deeply into what people meant by "seeing." Again, research indicated that visitors

defined the word as specifically as *Webster's* did, even when Museum staff did not. To learn is to discover, and to discover is to make visible for the first time. In fact, when visitors said they wanted "to see" they meant they wanted to <u>learn</u> about the Museum and its collection. The use of the verb "to see" was an accurate shorthand for their desire for a learning experience rather than an educational experience.

Both recreation and learning, then, were perceived as active pursuits, where the individual shaped the experience through the act of being restored or discovering new knowledge. In fact, the process of seeing and discovering in itself was a form of recreation for many of our visitors—a leisure learning experience. One visitor said of a visit to Winterthur that it was "such an incredibly rich experience for me . . . I go away feeling enlightened in a way that I rarely ever do in my day-to-day life. That's why for me it's the perfect getaway, the perfect vacation. I'm not turning my brain off . . . That's why I don't go to the Caribbean, I come to places like this."

The next question to consider is that once visitors have come to the Museum, many wanting active learning and recreational experiences, how are they "held"? In visitor studies, "holding" refers to the ability of an exhibition or object to engage a visitor mentally or physically for a length of time long enough for some cognitive or affective reaction. If visitors often are interested in discovering for themselves something about decorative arts, what are the ways they naturally go about this?

There are many methods used to try to help visitors with these cognitive and affective tasks. While some of these methods may be used in learning situations, they are developed for different purposes, such as Winterthur's own points of connoisseurship developed by Charles Montgomery for the appraisal of objects. Others, such as Bloom's taxonomy of thinking for formal educational settings, build upon a hierarchical approach to learning. Some, such as those that espouse helping visitors to "read an object," assume a mental similarity between the decoding of letters and words and the perception of tangible objects.[10]

At Winterthur, educators were well versed in these theories because they had been using them for years in public programming. During ERT research, however, the staff discovered that these theories did not match visitor reality. Visitors at Winterthur thought about decorative arts in a wholly different manner. They were "held" to an object by the use of one or more thinking strategies that are non-hierarchical and that are primary to human experience in the world.

In this research study,[11] visitor responses to a chair were grouped into like categories based upon the content of their answers. What emerged were four categories of thinking strategies (Figure 2). Responses were:

• description (based upon observable identifiable characteristics);

description

Count, recognize,
define, label, list
What is it made of?
What is it?

classification

Compare, analyze,
match, contrast
What style is it?
What date is it?

association

Imagine,
remember, speculate
Do you have one?
Who would use?

Choose, judge,
select, decide, prefer
Which do you like best?
Is it authentic?

evaluation

FIGURE 2: Wheel of Interpretation

The wheel is an alternative to hierarchical models of thinking strategies. When interpreters and visitors use the language listed under a heading, they are demonstrating that thinking strategy. The goal for interpreters is to begin where visitors are and then move to other sections to help visitors strengthen their perception skills in all four areas.

- classification (putting the object into a category based upon knowledge of other similar objects)—e.g., name, style;
- association (connecting the object in intangible ways with other objects, people or personal or historical events)—e.g., my grandmother has one, George Washington used one;
- evaluation (judging its authenticity, condition, value or aesthetics).

One surprising finding was that, in any group of visitors, all of the four strategies were present. Further, the variety of responses was not age-dependent. In interviews with preschoolers through senior citizens, visitors age seven and over used at

least one of these four basic ways to perceive an object. Despite the seemingly more complex skill educators traditionally attribute to categories like evaluation, there was no age relation that predicted where visitors might begin their journey. A hierarchy of thinking strategies did not exist. Why was that?

Neuroscience helps to explain how humans learn about and experience the world through visual perception and recognition of objects.[12] Perception is a physical sensation (often sight in a museum) interpreted in the light of experience. Unlike a reading metaphor that builds upon what's been labeled by reading specialists as a "relatively late cultural invention,"[13] even babies perceive decorative arts as they build their memory banks of objects in their homes. Thinking strategies used by museum visitors are complex interactions of their physical being with a material world and an ever-expanding memory of associations. In addition, thinking strategies are not biologically inscribed characteristics. People will use the strategy (or strategies) that best fits the mix of object before them and associative memories available at that point in their lives. People do, and can, use all four thinking strategies in one visit.

Overall, the conclusions of these studies of motivation to attend and learn in a decorative arts museum have taught the members of the ERT to be more respectful of the complexity of visitors' thinking strategies, to create experiences that allow individuals to be active participants and to respect the diversity of visitors' knowledge bases.

Respect for the complexity of thinking strategies in the visiting public includes respect for what seem to us, "the professionals," as simplistic, extraneous or incorrect responses. For example, upon entering a room of hundreds of objects set in an over-furnished colonial revival parlor, many a woman has exclaimed, "Who dusts all this?" In the past, unfortunately, guides mentally dismissed these visitors as not caring about the decorative arts. In fact, those visitors had been "grabbed" and "held" by that display. They had discovered for themselves the layers of physical complexity in a museum exhibition, and they related it to their own experiences as housekeepers. Such visitors are *perceiving* the objects, and guides may honor this cognitive and affective activity by providing a historical context about who and how these objects were used in the past. What seemed to be a "throw-away" response is an entrée into issues of interpreting and exhibiting decorative arts.

Secondly, museum experiences are being shaped to foster active participation. Interpretation is a conversation between the visitor and the object. In a museum like Winterthur, where guided tours are the most common way visitors encounter objects, the conversation also includes the guide. Guides are active participants in this three-way "discussion," not as facilitators but as one leg of a triangle where each member's contribution supports the other.

This definition of interpretation is not unlike Joseph Pine and James Gilmore's definition of the experience economy where services (guides, exhibitions) set the stage and goods (or objects) are props to "engage individual customers in a way that creates a memorable event." They define four broad categories of experience consumers desire (entertainment, education, escape and esthetic) that are somewhat similar to the motivations uncovered for museum visiting. The authors go further to indicate that entertainment is a passive activity while educational events (or according to ERT, learning events) call for more active involvement.[14]

Thirdly, even at a museum with a very traditional visitation like Winterthur, visitors are diverse in the experiences they wish to encounter and the ways in which they will perceive our objects. Preliminary research suggests that this type of diversity may cross education, gender or racial lines. People seem to arrive at the museum's door with a myriad of reasons for visiting; they think about objects using their varied and broad memory banks. How do museums shape interpretation then? How can they make the decorative arts meaningful and relevant without working with each visitor as an individual, something that flies in the face of practical logistics and visitor expectations of a social venture?

Fortunately, commonalities exist that help shape interpretation. In 1992, Winterthur published an interpretive goal for the Museum to help visitors understand the meanings that objects have in people's lives. Enriching this goal with current theories about visitors, new educational initiatives have begun to put theory into practice.

At Winterthur, because guided tours are currently the major form of interpreting the decorative arts to the public, guide training is extensive and paramount. A course entitled "Excellence in Interpretation" debuted in 1994 to help guides discover for themselves the diversity of visitors and to help the guides think actively about how to accommodate this diversity with respect. The course has not only been successful at Winterthur but has been offered at other historical and art museums in the mid-Atlantic region. Guides who have taken the course often say that the theories support their "gut" feelings about visitors; thus the course serves to increase the guides' self-respect as well.

The research also has informed work on non-guided exhibitions. Knowledge of the complexity of visitor responses encourages front-end and formative evaluation for exhibitions. In one recent case, that research was instrumental in writing a set of labels for the exhibition *KiDS! 200 Years of Childhood*. Front-end evaluation showed that visitors had very strong opinions about the history of childhood based upon their individual value systems. Mostly they thought that children today lived in a worse world, and were themselves worse beings, than children in the past. Winterthur as an institution did not want to tell people what they should believe, but it felt that it would be helpful for people, upon seeing the objects and learning of some of the realities of childhood in the past, to discuss this information among themselves in light of their values and memories. "Talk It Over" labels sprinkled throughout the show encourage intergenerational sharing on topics like what is important for children to learn morally and intellectually and whether gender-specific toys are necessary.

In summary, museum professionals in decorative arts museums should consider carefully the things visitors <u>do</u> in museums—they *look*, they *think*, they *see*. While visitors often seem to give facile answers to questions, they, in fact, are using statements of verbal precision and awesome complexity. What museum professionals, therefore, must be <u>doing</u> in museums is *listening* and *thinking* to build *understanding*.

ENDNOTES:

1. The Education Research Team (ERT) currently consists of Amber Auld Combs, Tracey Rae Beck, Pauline K. Eversmann, Debbie V. R. Harper, Rosemary T. Krill, Edwina Michael and the author. In January 2000, ERT changed its name to Visitor Research Team (VRT).

2. *The Handbook for Winterthur Interpreters: A Multidisciplinary Analysis of the Winterthur Collection* was created by a core of educators, many of whom later founded the ERT. The *Handbook*, first published in-house (Pauline K. Eversmann and Rosemary Troy Krill, Winterthur, Del.: Henry Francis du Pont Winterthur Museum, 1992), forms the basis for a forthcoming publication by Rosemary Troy Krill from AltaMira Press.

3. The early visitor research work of the Denver Art Museum is explained in McDermott, M. (1988), "Through Their Eyes: What Novices Value in Art Experiences." Martin Sullivan et. al., eds., *The Sourcebook*. Washington D.C.: American Association of Museums, 133-162. The Getty's informal focus group methodology was discussed in the "Formative Evaluation of Museum Technology" session of the 1996 American Association of Museums Annual Meeting in Minneapolis, Minnesota.

4. See Glaser, B. G. and Strauss, A. L. (1967). *The Discovery of Grounded Theory: Strategies for Qualitative Research*. New York: Aldine Publishing Co.

5. Many articles in the *Journal of Museum Education, Visitor Behavior* (later *Visitor Studies*) and *Curator* as well as papers presented at the American Association of Museum's "Learning in Museums" seminars discuss why people attend museums and what they learn. In addition, the ERT found Marilyn G. Hood's dissertation, "Adult Attitudes Toward Leisure Choices in Relation to Museum Participation" (Ph.D. dissertation, Ohio State University, 1981) very helpful. The metaphor "reading an object" has permeated the museum education field since the mid-1970s. For one explanation, see Rice, D. (1988). "Vision and Culture: The Role of Museums in Visual Literacy." *Journal of Museum Education* 13, no. 3, Fall, 13-17.

6. The ideas of attracting, holding and communicating to visitors, while not unique, formed the basis of the Visitor Studies Association workshop "Overview of Exhibit Evaluation and Critical Appraisal" conducted by Stephen Bitgood and Harris Shettel in Washington D.C., August 1998.

7. For discussions of this dichotomy, see Beeho, A. J. and Prentice, R. C. (1995). "Evaluating the Experiences and Benefits Gained by Tourists Visiting a Socio-Industrial Heritage Museum: An Application of ASEB Grid Analysis at Blists Hill Open-Air Museum." *Museum Management and Curatorship*. 14: 229-251 and Falk, J. H. (1998). "Visitors: Who Comes, Who Doesn't and Why?" *Museum News* 77: 38-43.

8. For details of the research project's methodology and conclusions, see Combs, A. A. "Why Do They Come? Listening to Visitors' Voices at a Decorative Arts Museum." *Curator* 42:3 (forthcoming).

9. All dictionary definitions come from (1987). *Webster's Ninth New Collegiate Dictionary*. Springfield, Mass.: Merriam-Webster Inc., Publishers.

10. Montgomery's 14 points of connoisseurship were originally published in (1961). "Some Remarks on the Science and Principles of Connoisseurship." *Walpole Society Notebook*. For an explanation of Bloom's taxonomy of thinking skills, read Sprinthall, N. A. and Sprinthall, R. C., eds. (1990). *Education Psychology: A Developmental Approach*. New York: McGraw-Hill, 350-356.

11. The methodology and conclusions of the entire research project are published as Eversmann, Pauline K., Rosemary T. Krill, Edwina Michael, Beth A. Twiss-Garrity and Tracey Rae Beck. (1997). "Material Culture as Text: Review and Reform of the Literacy Model for Interpretation." *American Material Culture: The Shape of the Field*. Winterthur, DE: Henry Francis du Pont Winterthur Museum, 135-167.

12. Two good summaries of neuroscience as it relates to learning are Kosslyn, S. M. and Koenig, O. (1992). *Wet Mind: The New Cognitive Neuroscience*. New York: Free Press and Falk, J. H. (1996). "Recent Advances in the Neurosciences: Implications for Visitor Studies." *Visitor Studies: Theory, Research and Practice*. 9, 228-238.

13. Lytle, S. L. and Botel, M. (1990). *The Pennsylvania Framework for Reading, Writing, and Talking Across the Curriculum*. Harrisburg: Pennsylvania Department of Education, 21.

14. Pine, II, J. and Gilmore, J. H. (1998) "Welcome to the Experience Economy." *Harvard Business Review*. July-August, 97-105. Their theories are applied to museums by Kotler, N. (1999). "Delivering Experience: Marketing the Museum's Full Range of Assets." *Museum News*. May/June, 30-39, 58-61.

Catch the FU▣ in

A BASEBALL MITT ARMCHAIR?

A CACTUS COATRACK?

FU▣KY FURNISHINGS!

A VOLCANO LAMP?

A CRICKET TELEPHONE?

GALLERY TOUR:
Play ball!
Enjoy FU▣ activities
in the exhibition
Masterworks:
Italian Design, 1960–1994

DESIGN WORKSHOP
Light up your night games!
Create your own FU▣ky
nightlight with industrial
designer Maximillian Burton
of Smart Design, Inc.

Both Grown-ups'
and Children's
Programs at the

BGC

for young people
ages 6 to 12
and their
adult companions

Design(ing) Literacy: How to Make It Happen?

Lisa Podos, Director of Public Programs
The Bard Graduate Center for Studies in the Decorative Arts

Introduction:

This group of papers will examine the designing of "design literacy." In considering "how to make it happen?," the question mark will be interpreted as a signifier of both the attendant issues and proposed strategies for realizing this objective. The three authors—Philip Yenawine, Co-Director of Visual Understanding in Education and former Director of Education at the Museum of Modern Art (MoMA); Lisa Podos, Director of Public Programs at The Bard Graduate Center for Studies in the Decorative Arts (BGC); and Julie Trager, Adjunct Lecturer at California State University Los Angeles and East Los Angeles College, former member of MoMA's Department of Education and Consultant to the BGC— became associated in the process of developing educational programs at the BGC.[1]

The BGC is a young institution, founded in 1993, located in New York City, and affiliated with Bard College in upstate New York. The mission of the center is to increase knowledge and appreciation of the decorative arts and design. To this end, the BGC offers M.A. and Ph.D. degree-granting programs of study, mounts several exhibitions annually, houses an extensive library and publishes a scholarly journal.

In addition, the BGC organizes a variety of exhibition-related and general-interest public programs for visitors with backgrounds ranging from professionals in the arts, design and architecture to walk-in visitors and ages spanning from senior citizens to young children.

The BGC programs for youth audiences focus on a category that traditionally has been called "family programs," connoting intergenerational events generally held on weekends and during after-school hours for parents and their offspring. Concerns that arose in conceptualizing these offerings—given the statistical obsolescence of this familial designation and the demographics of the local population—impelled the BGC to coin a more inclusive programmatic name for these offerings.[2] The result, Both Grown-ups' and Children's (BGC) Programs at the BGC (see photo on previous page), is specifically worded:

- to omit the term "graduate" in order to prevent confusion as to why programs for youngsters are being offered at a graduate school;
- to avoid the word "studies" since the goal is to suggest that these programs are leisure activities as well as educational;
- to exclude any reference to "family" and thereby suggest a more inclusive audience than the traditional designation of this term;
- and, most important, to stress both grown-ups and children since the programs are designed for children to participate along with their adult companions.

The formation of BGC Programs at the BGC grew out of research undertaken for a thesis I wrote for the Bank Street Graduate School of Education's Leadership in Museum Education program. Entitled *The Decorative Arts Question*,[3] this study assessed the potential of applying the pioneering work initiated by Philip Yenawine and his colleagues at MoMA from fine arts to decorative arts education.[4] Yenawine and Trager both were instrumental in the process of determining valid applications, and their input remains valuable as the resulting programs evolve.[5]

This group of papers reviews the ongoing process of exploring "the decorative arts question." Yenawine's paper begins with an outline of the theory of aesthetic development and its implications for visual thinking and literacy. My paper will examine the goals of the BGC Programs at the BGC, with reference to the application of visual thinking strategies. Trager's paper will consider the successes and problems we have faced at the BGC in adapting visual thinking strategies to decorative arts education, and will offer suggestions for the future refinement of such programs.

ENDNOTES:

1. This paper is a revised version of my comments presented in the session given jointly with Julie Trager and Philip Yenawine at the symposium *Old Collections, New Audiences: Decorative Arts and the Visitor Experience for the 21st Century*, November 12, 1999.

2. For instance, Borun, M. et. al. (1995). "Family Learning in Museums: A Bibliographic Review" in *Curator: The Museum Journal* 38 (4), pp. 262-270, cited a study in which only nine percent of families of the United States were found to represent the conventional definition of a nuclear family comprising two parents and two to five shared children.

3. Podos, L. (1998). *The Decorative Arts Question: A Study of the Development of Both Grown-ups' and Children's Programs at The Bard Graduate Center*, unpublished thesis, Leadership in Museum Education Program, Bank Street College Graduate School of Education.

4. In the 1980s, Yenawine commissioned a study by cognitive psychologist Abigail Housen that served as the basis for the Visual Thinking Curriculum (VTC) methodology used at MoMA for fine arts education. Refer to his paper on "Housen's Theory of Aesthetic Development" in this volume for a discussion of the underlying stage theory and its implications. See also his discussion of a variant methodology, the Visual Thinking Strategies (VTS).

5. I also would like to acknowledge the contributions of Cynthia Nachmani, Coordinator of School Programs at MoMA, whose ongoing constructive feedback has contributed greatly to the development of BGC Programs at the BGC. Nachmani currently is spearheading an evaluation of the VTC's educational impact being implemented by Harvard Project Zero, a research organization at the Harvard Graduate School of Education. It is interesting to note that some of the findings and recommendations submitted in their analysis support the modifications to the methodology adopted at the BGC. Additionally, I would like to thank Dorothy Dunn, Head of Education, Cooper-Hewitt, National Design Museum, Smithsonian Institution, for her insightful recommendations and inspirational work.

Housen's Theory and Decorative Arts Education

Philip Yenawine, Co-Director
Visual Understanding in Education

The most useful information I have encountered during my 30 years as a museum educator has been that produced by Abigail Housen, a cognitive psychologist whose research and theories focus on art. Housen was initially intrigued by the observation that some people know nothing about art while others are experts; since experts must have once been naive, they had undergone many changes as their capacities and stores of information grew. Housen wanted to understand the nature of those changes: how, when and why do aesthetic processes and concepts develop? Since the mid-1970s, she has conducted many careful, detailed studies to explore these questions, and her interpretations of findings have serious implications for museum education.

Housen began her research by observing the behaviors of museum visitors. Soon she wanted to know what thoughts motivated those behaviors. As her interest built, she realized that understanding the spectrum of viewers would involve studying people of diverse ages, backgrounds, educations and economic levels, not just those who visit museums.

In collecting information concerning this range of viewers, Housen paid particular attention to the practices of developmental psychology. Examining her data, she began to believe that a stage theory—often the result of developmental research—could be applied to aesthetic change. She examined various writings on aesthetics and perception, and found that her growing insights resonated with the findings of others. She also discovered that while the thoughts of experienced viewers were often studied and discussed in the literature, those of naive viewers were less understood.

After nearly five years of research to develop a methodology, collect data, interpret findings and begin drawing theoretical conclusions, Housen published a study on the subject of aesthetic development in 1979. She went on to conduct further tests of her method, collect additional profiles and make more detailed analyses of findings. In 1983, she submitted her doctoral thesis, which included a "coding manual" that detailed her method of analyzing aesthetic thought, to the Harvard Graduate School of Education. The manual is a compendium of thoughts collected from interviews with individuals viewing works of art. A thought is categorized in two ways: first, according to its specific characteristics, and then according to its context in patterns of thinking. Housen also presented a well-documented theory of how aesthetic thinking progresses through stages.

Housen's primary data collection tool is a non-directive, stream-of-consciousness interview. Participants are asked simply to talk about anything they see as they look at a work of art, to say whatever comes into their minds. There are no directed questions or other prompts to influence the viewer's process. Called the Aesthetic Development Interview, or ADI, this provides Housen with a window into a person's thinking processes. In addition to being empirical, it minimizes researcher biases or assumptions.

After a very detailed, thought-by-thought analysis, Housen studies each interview as a totality to see how individual thoughts fit into an overall context. Finally, she factors in demographic, attitudinal and biographical information about each interviewee, as well as her/his responses to specific questions. From all of this, she is able to assign an aesthetic stage to the interview. To date, Housen and her associates have coded over 6,000 ADIs taken from individuals ranging from six-year-old children to eighty-something adults of both genders; these people run the spectrum in terms of art experience, race, ethnicity, education and economic status.

A wide variety of art has been used for the ADIs but virtually all of it has been in the categories of painting, sculpture and the like. These works have what I refer to as "expressive content": emotional content is usually embedded alongside more objective information. Ambiguity and layers of meaning leave room for multiple interpretations. The data, therefore, is less certainly applicable to viewers' experience of works of decorative arts than to these other categories.

Over the course of years, Housen identified five distinct patterns of thinking about art, which she described as aesthetic stages:

Stage I:

Accountive viewers are storytellers. Using their senses, memories and personal associations, they make concrete observations about a work of art that are woven into a narrative. Here, judgments are based on what is known and what is liked. Emotions color their comments, as viewers seem to enter the work of art and become part of its unfolding narrative.

Stage II:

Constructive viewers set about building a framework for looking at works of art, using the most logical and accessible tools: their own perceptions, their knowledge of the natural world, and the values of their social, moral and conventional world. If the work does not look the way it is "supposed to"—if craft, skill, technique, hard work, utility and function are not evident, or if the subject seems inappropriate—then these viewers judge the work to be "weird," lacking or of no value. Their sense of what is realistic is the standard often applied to determine value. As emotions begin to go underground, these viewers begin to distance themselves from the work of art.

Stage III:

Classifying viewers adopt the analytical and critical stance of the art historian. They want to identify the work as to place, school, style, time and provenance. They decode the work using their library of facts and figures that they are ready and eager to expand. This viewer believes that, properly categorized, the work of art's meaning and message can be explained and rationalized.

Stage IV:

Interpretive viewers seek a personal encounter with a work of art. Exploring the work and letting its meaning slowly unfold, they appreciate subtleties of line and shape and color. Now, critical skills are put in the service of feelings and intuitions as these viewers let underlying meanings of the work—what it symbolizes—emerge. Each new encounter with a work of art presents a chance for new comparisons, insights and experiences. Knowing that the work of art's identity and value are subject to reinterpretation, these viewers see their own processes subject to chance and change.

Stage V:

Re-creative viewers, having a long history of viewing and reflecting about works of art, now "willingly suspend disbelief." A familiar painting is like an old friend who is known intimately, yet full of surprise, deserving attention on a daily level but also existing on an elevated plane. As in all-important friendships, time is a key ingredient, allowing Stage V viewers to know the ecology of a work—its time, its history, its questions, its travels, its intricacies. Drawing on their own history with one work in particular, and with viewing in general, these viewers combine personal contemplation with views that broadly encompass universal concerns. Here, memory infuses the landscape of the painting, intricately combining the personal and the universal.

   Significant to understanding aesthetic development is that, while growth is related to age, it is not determined by it. A person of any age with no experience with art will necessarily be in Stage I; an adult will not be at a higher stage than a child simply by virtue of age. A good education does not ensure a higher stage, unless it has involved direct experience with visual art. Exposure to art over time is the only way to develop, and without time and exposure, aesthetic development does not occur.

Over the course of her studies, Housen has found that most interviewees are beginner viewers, in Stages I and II. Even among frequent museum goers, there are relatively few people who have had sufficient interaction with art to have developed beyond the understandings of Stage II/III (which is a transition between two stages, II and III). Very few are Stages III and beyond, and virtually all of these are arts professionals of one sort or another. Housen refers to the majority of the Stage I and II viewers as "beginners" because their behaviors lie below a threshold of literacy that one might call "functional." They have a still-limited ability to find meaning in a range of art; they are short of the kind of fluency that, in reading, would be represented by flexibility in understanding and enjoying prose, poetry and expository writing of varying styles and content.

Given that the research has been conducted without a focus on the decorative arts, what conclusions may we draw from the data to guide thinking about education in this area? One helpful insight results from a study among elementary students who were in a long-term study of aesthetic development and its transfer. In this instance, in addition to ADIs, students looked at other kinds of objects (mostly artifacts: a foreign coin, a mortar and pestle, an anemometer, a fossil) and were asked open-ended questions about what they saw. Over the course of the five-year study, students grew from a mean score of Stage I to a mean of Stage II, with half of the students therefore in the upper reaches of Stage II, and some of them in the transition stage, Stage II/III. All the while, students showed growth in their viewing skills as applied to "expressive art." There was, however, no consistent, general transfer of these viewing skills to objects of material culture until Stage II; before that Stage, there were minor indications that some progress was being made, but nothing significant. This suggests that, before Stage II, the viewing skills most helpful for appreciating decorative arts are nascent, though not clearly in place.

Looking at this phenomenon in light of the stage descriptions above is illuminating. Stage I viewers' strength is using random and relatively sparse observations, all based on prior knowledge of their world (which has included little or no art) to draw some kind of story from an image. They do this no matter what they examine: paintings by Hopper or Cezanne, African figures, abstractions. As a meaning-making system, this has limited usefulness with many of the things studied in decorative arts, though to the extent that furniture and decorative artifacts tell a story, or do so in the context in which they are seen, the instinctual behaviors of Stage I viewers can reasonably apply.

Stage II viewers bring many more interests and skills to the experience of viewing decorative arts. They are impressed by craftsmanship. They become interested in how things come to look as they do, and, at some point, in how they are made. Elements of design slowly develop as interests for Stage II viewers. Questions of function can intrigue. This is a very "educable" stage.

Stage III is where matters of classification, maker, history and condition become the focus of the viewer, and it is at this stage that such data becomes memorable. Before this point, although it is possible for the motivated to memorize facts, information is not necessarily used well by the viewer. It might well be misunderstood and misapplied. Information might help one make sense of one thing, but not necessarily others.

Serious connoisseurship, such as being able to assign quality with assurance, understand deeper implications of a given work or style and converse deeply and broadly about the meanings of objects and their contexts, does not happen before Stage IV.

Housen and I have worked together for almost ten years, developing a teaching strategy that applies her theories to teaching. The program we have designed is called Visual Thinking Strategies (VTS). The VTS is designed to address the interests and strengths of viewers in Stage I and early Stage II, and to follow their developmental arc, supporting and challenging them appropriately. For example, in order to make the most of beginning viewers' storytelling facility, the VTS emphasizes narrative art at the outset. The teaching method centers on questions: What is going on in this image? What do you see that makes you say that? What more can you find? Teachers are taught ways of responding to student comments supportively and facilitating the ensuing discussions.

The VTS is being used in museums and in schools with impressive results not only in developing viewing skills but also in advancing other thinking and communication skills. The results indicate that students can be functioning in Stage II as early as fifth grade, and therefore, are primed for programs that focus on the decorative arts. Elsewhere in this publication, you will find educators discussing their use of the VTS in the teaching programs of decorative arts institutions, tailoring it to assist with specific goals of their programs.

Exploring the Decorative Arts Question at The Bard Graduate Center

Lisa Podos, Director of Public Programs
The Bard Graduate Center for Studies in the Decorative Arts

VTC to BGC:

Learning of the work done at MoMA and seeing the Visual Thinking Curriculum (VTC) in action, I became convinced that a questioning strategy based on aesthetic stage theory was a viable structure upon which to build an inquiry-based decorative arts education methodology. Accordingly, I set out to create a program that would accomplish a two-part goal:

(1) Intellectual: to further an understanding of our past and present material culture; and

(2) Developmental: to encourage the maturation of analytical and verbal skills in youth, and ultimately all age audiences, through observation and discussion of something we all share in our lives that can be interpreted both personally and culturally—namely design. The challenge was how to adapt the VTC from fine arts to decorative arts in terms of content, process and context.

In contemplating these issues, the following concerns regarding content, process and context were paramount:

Content: Could the questioning strategy validly be adapted from fine arts to decorative arts?

- Does looking at inherently functional objects make open-ended questions invalid, since there are "right" answers?

- Is it, therefore, necessary to supply information? If so, how do educators do that without becoming fact-based lecturers giving historical data?

- Do visitors bring a different set of expectations to viewing decorative arts as compared to fine arts objects?

Process: Could the questioning strategy be successfully adapted from narrative, sequenced material to non-narrative, non-sequenced material?

- Does the developmental aesthetic stage theory apply in the same way to the decorative arts as the fine arts? If so, are most decorative arts viewers at the novice level (Stages I and II)? Similarly, are there significant differences between adult and youth viewers of decorative arts objects?

- Can Stage I (accountive) viewers be engaged in looking at decorative arts objects or must questions be targeted directly to Stage III (classifying) viewers and thereby deal with facts, such as the importance of function?

- How can mixed-level groups be accommodated without talking down to novice viewers, for example asking "What do you see?" in front of a table?

Context: Could the questioning strategy be meaningfully adapted from academic programs for students and their teachers to informal situations with intergenerational audiences?

- How can parents and other caregivers be trained to become active, engaged and empowered to look at design this way without an arts educator facilitating?

- If the need for some external information is acknowledged, can independent adult buy-in be feasible?

- Is the methodology transferable to adult/child discourse outside of the arts? If so, does it enhance making connections in and among other domains?

In resolving these issues, the BGC Programs at the BGC were developed.

BGC Programs at the BGC:

BGC Programs at the BGC target 6- to 12-year-old children with their adult companions. The middle years group was selected based on the appropriate cognitive skills of youngsters at this age. Moreover, this is an age range during which adults are searching for stimulating activities to share with their children.

The multi-component format of a single event includes an interactive guided tour, a themed refreshment break and a hands-on design workshop. Each segment, particularly the tour, depends on an inquiry-driven dialogue. The core of the methodology is the Decorative Arts Questioning Strategy (DAQS).

The DAQS was inspired by the VTC questioning strategy, which advocates grounded observations to construct meaning. The questions do differ from the core VTC questions in several important respects. Fundamentally, they derive from the premise that some information must be given to the audience and that they deal with multiple issues. For instance, Question 2 assumes that details regarding the function of an object are provided and Questions 3 and 4 delve into analytical interpretations of meaning.

Furthermore, the multi-component format in which the DAQS is applied deviates from the VTC curriculum. Recognizing the validity of alternative educational theories, different segments are planned to engage other learning modalities besides visual and verbal, and to access the multiple intelligences posited by Howard Gardner.[1] The overall constructivist approach to educational experiences accords with the work of George Hein, Lynn Dierking, John Falk and other current theorists and practitioners in the field.[2]

Case Study—FUNky Furnishings:

The format and strategies of a BGC Program at the BGC will be exemplified herein by a typical offering, FUNky Furnishings. This event was conceived to complement the exhibition *Masterworks: Italian Design, 1960–1994.*[3] To make the exhibition content accessible to younger audiences, the theme that design can be FUN as well as FUNctional was developed and participants were encouraged to "catch the FUN in FUNky Furnishings!"[4] This theme fulfilled the aim of all BGC exhibition-related educational offerings: to connect what is seen on the exhibition visit to the real life experiences of the visitor.[5]

The basic components of this event described as follows are representative of BGC Programs at the BGC.

Arrival (5 minutes):

Each participant received a nametag, a schedule for the afternoon, and an activity box including:

- activity guide designed for use on the tour with the DAQS and/or for self-guided tours;
- oversize pencil;
- colored pencils;
- other information relevant to the tour and/or used for planned activities;
- BGC Programs at the BGC sticker;
- evaluation for either adults or children;
- pass for a return visit to the BGC;
- DAQS handout for adults only.

Tour (55 minutes):

The participants were separated into groups with a maximum of 15 participants per group, roughly divided by age, 6-8 or 9-12, and accompanying adults. Each group was taken around the exhibition by an arts educator in a generally predetermined circuit focusing on objects selected to engage the viewers based on the programmatic theme. The guides employed the DAQS and activity guide to facilitate engagement with the objects and among the visitors.

The text of the activity guide was written to provide visitors with a starting point for their own explorations. The order of the text was loosely based on developmental aesthetic stage theory: the user was encouraged to begin with egocentric investigation, move to their own environment and then progress to the external world. The carefully sequenced questions supported by factual and "fun" information along with writing and drawing exercises were intended to offer what interpretive specialist Marlene Chambers calls "a discovery opportunity" which will "give…visitors a sense of being competent and in control and a chance to find new, personally significant insights…(as) these feelings of satisfaction—not the information learned—motivate the repeat experience and continued learning." The actual design of the piece demarcates the breakdown of questions, information and activities: questions are stated in a large point size and black lettering, supplemental information is in sidebars and exercises are on a lighter green ground.

After the cover, the sequence and focus of the pages are:

2: *The Home Team:* why objects we live with look the way they do

3: *A Double Play:* design choices in relation to function and form

4: *Major League Material:* man-made and natural materials

5: *Sitting on the Bench:* seating

6: *Game Highlights:* lighting

7: *A Pop Hit:* design inspiration, especially in relation to popular culture, and designing a piece of furniture

8: *Extra Innings:* suggestions for follow-up projects to be done at home and other museums

Themed Refreshment and Reference Materials (15 minutes):

Following the exhibition tour, all participants joined together for a refreshment break. This transition period was used as an opportunity to stimulate different senses in support of the theme. The snack food was linked to the program theme—both visually with red and green M & Ms echoing the colors of the activity guide, which were selected as the national colors of Italy, and in terms of taste with biscotti being served as representative of Italian fare. While enjoying these treats, participants looked on their own through reference materials, including the exhibition catalogue and assorted books on topics such as design in the home, inventions of synthetic materials like plastics and the culture of Italy.

Design Workshop (75 minutes):

After the refreshment break, the group moved to the design workshop in which industrial designer Maximillian Burton of Smart Design led everyone in making nightlights that were both FUN and FUNctional. Each participant received the materials to make their own nightlight; however, the project was planned to promote collaboration. Associated intergenerational units were encouraged to choose a symbol to link their designs. Grown-ups and children had to work together in the process of crafting and gluing their creations.

The materials available to fabricate the nightlights were inspired by the objects on view in the exhibition, but made contemporary and relevant to the participants. The budding industrial designers joined pieces of brightly colored plastics into a whimsical shape or box and then affixed materials gathered from establishments such as the Coca-Cola, Disney and Nike stores; New York City cultural organizations; and current periodicals in order to personalize their nightlight. These found objects were selected to epitomize 1990s popular culture, just as the postwar Italian objects had reflected the pop culture of their era. The finished assemblage was glued to a nightlight base. Plugged in at home, each creation was meant to remind participants of the presence of design in their daily life.

Follow-up Training for Adults at MoMA:

To augment the experience at the BGC, a follow-up training session for adults was offered at MoMA. The goal of this session was to model the looking and questioning process and give older participants a chance to practice the DAQS. Each grown-up attendee received an invitation to attend what was promoted as an educational and social event.

At MoMA, the program began with a reception over which MoMA and BGC staff presented the background of the VTC and DAQS in order to provide the adults with a rationale for accepting this pedagogical approach. The group then went on a carefully sequenced tour of objects in the permanent collection, beginning in the cafeteria looking at lighting to reinforce the message that design is all around us every day. By the end of the session, almost every participant had led a portion of the tour by asking questions and encouraging discussion in front of one of the pieces. Each adult received a pass to return with their children so they could replicate the tour experience on their own.

Program Evaluation:

The feedback to BGC Programs at the BGC has been overwhelmingly positive. The events are consistently sold out. Moreover, the high frequency of return visits establishes that these offerings are popular with participants.

While no longitudinal or quantitative studies of participant experiences have been performed, evaluations have provided some valuable qualitative data regarding attendance motivations. Furthermore, there is some indication of take-away learning. Excerpts from select evaluations substantiate these affirmative responses, as follows:

Grown-ups:

Question: Why did attending this event appeal to you?

Response: I like furniture design and felt it was more interesting for a child than going to a regular museum.

Question: What kind of experiences did you hope you and/or your child would gain from this event?

Response: See the world in a new way.

Question: Did the event provide you with any concepts or skills you can practice at home with your children?

Response: Making us aware that design is all around us.

Children:

Question: What did you learn?

Response: I learned how to look at furnishings in a different way.

Other evaluations, however, not only commented on the successes of the program but raised some limitations. When asked "Did the event provide you with any concepts or skills you can practice at home with your children?," one adult responded, "It did, but we won't. We need this type of experience where you prepare everything for us." This attitude is fundamentally at odds with the premise of the DAQS and the objectives of BGC Programs at the BGC, and must be addressed.

Conclusion:

BGC Programs at the BGC are modeling an active and engaging looking, listening and thinking experience. Now, it must be determined whether this experience is empowering. Ultimately, are these programs design(ing) literacy?

ENDNOTES:

1. For further information on the MI theory, refer to Gardner, H. (1983), *Frames of Mind: The Theory of Multiple Intelligences*, New York: BasicBooks, Harper Collins, as well as his more recent publications.

2. One of the most useful discussions of constructivism in terms of the educational experience in the museum is Hein, G. (1995), "The Constructivist Museum" in *Journal of Education in Museums*, 16, 21-23. See also Falk, J.H. and Dierking, L.D. (1992), *The Museum Experience*, Washington, D.C.: Whalesback Books, and (1991), "Redefining the Museum Experience: The Interactive Experience Model" in *Visitor Studies: Theory, Research, and Practice* 4, 173-176.

3. *Masterworks: Italian Design, 1960–1994* was an exhibition drawn from the collection of the Denver Art Museum and circulated by the American Federation of Arts that was on view at the BGC from April 11 until August 10, 1997. Both the DAM guest curator, R. Craig Miller, and his curatorial assistant, Carla Hartman, were helpful in providing materials and information to the BGC.

4. All BGC Programs at the BGC are thematically based. Note that studies cited by Bonnie Pittman-Gelles (1989), *Museums, Magic and Children*, Washington, D. C.: Association of Science Technology Centers, have established that thematic exhibition walk-throughs are more effective in reaching audiences than general walk-throughs. Empirical evidence at the BGC supports this conclusion.

5. Numerous analyses have indicated that learning is facilitated when such museum/life connections can be made; for example, refer to LaVilla-Havelin, J. S. (1989), "Family Learning in Museums" in B. Butler and M. Sussman (Eds.), *Museum Visits and Activities for Family Life Enrichment*, New York and London: Haworth Press, 87-99.

6. See Chambers, M. (1988), "Improving the Esthetic Experience for Art Novices: A New Paradigm for Interpretive Labels" in *AAM 1988 Annual Meeting Program Sourcebook*, Washington, D.C.: American Association of Museums.

Setting the Stage for Decorative Arts Education

Julie Trager, Adjunct Lecturer
California State University Los Angeles and East Los Angeles College

The years I spent at the Museum of Modern Art (MoMA) were vital years. It was during this time that the research of Abigail Housen was presented to the Education Department of MoMA and the seeds were planted for her collaboration with Philip Yenawine. The result of this collaboration was the Visual Thinking Curriculum (VTC). I was fortunate to observe and participate in the pilot stage and growth of this project. Socratic methodology and the stages of cognitive growth based on Piaget's and Housen's theories informed my methodology and growth as an educator. However, some of the underlying concepts of the VTC, reflecting Housen's research, were not as convincing to me when taken out of a theoretical context and brought into practice. The concerns which I initially had remain and permeate the issues Lisa Podos and I have addressed in applying the concepts of the VTC to decorative arts education in the "Both Grown-ups' and Children's Programs" at The Bard Graduate Center (also known as the BGC Programs at the BGC). This paper will address these concerns, the process of implementing the BGC Programs at the BGC, and the questions that remain today.

This project forced me to rethink what I had been doing, to evaluate what was effective about my methodology, and to consider how I could alter and manipulate what I found successful in the VTC. It forced me to find some concrete alternative solutions to those parts of the VTC that I had doubted. For instance, educators using the VTC ask their students a series of set questions that seem to apply only to narrative works in a familiar context.[1] We felt it was necessary to adjust the content of these questions to make them applicable to the decorative arts. Another concern was applying the Decorative Arts Questioning Strategy (DAQS)[2] to family groups attending single sessions where there was no assurance of repetitive encounters with the same families. We wanted the DAQS to have a lasting effect beyond our personal encounter with the families.

In a sense what we were asking was: What would be the richest viewing experience for children who were with us for just a few hours in a decorative arts museum, but in the best case scenario would return to BGC Programs at the BGC year after year? What could we do that would be lasting, beyond having a fun time, that would be meaningful, staying with the families after they left the Museum's doors? How could we instill in them a comfort level with decorative art objects, demystify the museum experience, and give visitors confidence to regard their own thoughts about the objects as valid? How could we give our audience tools and skills for looking and encourage critical and creative thinking so that the viewers would become self-sufficient decorative arts museumgoers? Could this be accomplished while incorporating information into the DAQS? How could we incorporate knowledge into the Socratic methodology, keeping in mind Piaget's theories, Housen's research and the VTC?

In trying to achieve this we have encountered successes and limitations. Over the past few years, BGC Programs at the BGC have been undeniably successful in terms of attendance, enjoyment by the visitors and repeat visits. Programs are always sold out and often we have had to create an additional day to accommodate the overflow. There has been positive response from the children and their adult friends as well as from newspapers in New York City, whose articles encourage the public to participate in these activities. BGC programs have also been a model for programs at peer institutions.

As I mentioned, since the inception of the BGC Programs at the BGC we have refined our initial model. A critical issue that we considered from the start was whether design objects demand external information. Would it compromise the meaning and intent of the design object if we did not discuss its context and cultural significance? How would we do this? Was it possible to create questions that could weave in information and encourage the looking process at the same time? We understood that this idea was contrary to the VTC stage theory. Since both of us were well versed in the VTC questioning strategy and respected and believed in its premise for the fine arts, we were now in a quandary as to how to create a model for a looking process that could be used in viewing design objects.

In the model we developed, the structure of the exhibition tour has become an important aspect and tool for the viewer to acquire knowledge. As in setting the stage for a theater production, the introduction—like the opening scene—presents the context of objects through directed questions, planting seeds for thoughts that are revealed during the process of exploring the exhibition. The introduction begins with a series of questions that are repeated in front of the objects throughout the course of the exhibition tour. These questions are focused to create an underlying theme that reflects the museum educator's concept of the exhibition. These additional questions, beyond the general DAQS, are tailored directly to each specific exhibition. Of course, when selecting the overall theme or main idea of the tour, the educator must consider what she or he wants the audience to think about when they leave the Museum.

The exhibition tour most often begins with a question that relates to the children's lives in the hope of creating a concrete connection between their own experiences and the exhibition. One might say that this is used as a "hook" to create natural and familiar associations with the ideas in the exhibition, and to encourage a comfort level within the Museum and acknowledge "what they already know." This is perhaps a point where we both meet and part with the VTC, for we use "what they already know" as a springboard to expand and apply cultural connections and information in the exhibition tour. We are not emphasizing Stage I of Housen's theory but rather focusing our visitors on Stages II and III, believing it is possible to go directly into analyzing the objects. We are asking our audience to create links by comparing what they already know with a different culture or historic period as a way of learning about the decorative arts. We hope to have the viewer understand that there is information imbedded in objects and that design is made in a context. This strategy is a means to an end—creating an awareness that design surrounds us in our everyday environment.

The choice of objects also is extremely important, each being like a character on a stage. As in a play, the dialogue between the objects helps to build a richer understanding of the individual pieces, as well as reveal their place within a context. As in our program "FUN Furnishings," for example, families began to look at materials, forms and functions of the objects as if they were archeologists. We repeatedly analyzed how function + form = design and how this equation tells us about the lifestyle and interests of the people who make and use these furnishings; that is, the decorative arts allow us to peek into another time and place. At this point, the viewer begins to obtain knowledge through his or her own exploration and build connections, weaving together the overall concept and theme of the exhibition tour. This experience is guided by the museum educator who operates as a facilitator or, using my analogy of theater, as a stage director.

This methodology demands that the museum educator be knowledgeable about the material and so comfortable with this knowledge that she or he is able to "let go" of preconceived notions about the objects and be open to varied responses from the audience. His or her ability to follow the lead of the audience is essential. While certain objects are highlighted because they are lead characters, secondary players may also be called on to tell the story. Within the overall theme, flexibility is necessary. The educator must adjust to the energy, expertise, age and interests of each particular group. No exhibition visit is ever the same.

In preparation for every new program, we give training workshops to our exhibition tour guides. It is at this time that we brainstorm how the specific decorative art objects on view can be connected with the children's own lives. Training sessions have always been a part of the VTC, but the format we have instituted diverges from the VTC training in that our workshops explore both how to apply questioning strategies and what information to build into the tour. These workshops have been very successful. Our guides, many of whom have been with us for several years, definitely have shown growth in applying this methodology, thus validating the idea that repetition is important to the learning process.

As mentioned, we believe that for our model to work, it is necessary to train the children's adult companions and empower them to apply the DAQS that encourages looking and talking about their surroundings wherever they are. To this end, we have offered workshops for accompanying grown-ups. While the few workshops we offered engaged the adults and some even successfully used our model, attendance was low, even when we tried different times of day and included a reception. Based on the merit of this concept, we still want to solve the problem of how to entice adults to a workshop without their children, a workshop that will enhance their long-term experience of looking at design.

At the BGC, we continuously question what will make people want to return to a decorative arts museum. What will make people pay closer attention to the objects that surround them, thereby bringing enriched meaning into their lives? We have learned that the VTC model does not exactly apply to design objects, although its questioning strategy is useful. We have successfully used design as a means of encouraging active looking, talking and thinking. We have discovered that additional information when viewing the decorative arts does facilitate a more meaningful experience. Now we need to determine: Can this model be employed at other museums? How do we build on what we know is successful as demonstrated by empirical evidence and make it work on a broader and more long-term basis? How can the DAQS further impact the lives of decorative arts museum viewers? Where do we go from here?

ENDNOTES:

1. Some of the main questions of the VTC and the VTS curriculums include: What is going on in this picture? What else is happening? Does someone see something different? What makes you say that?

2. Lisa Podos of the BGC authored these Suggested Questioning Strategies for Viewing and Discussing Decorative Art Objects in 1996:

What do you see?
    —What can you say about the color, line, shape, materials, and texture of this object?

What function do you think this object might serve or have served?
    —Who do you think might use or have used this object?
    —How might you use this object?
    —What do you see that makes you say that?

How, if at all, do you think the way this object looks relates to its use?
    —What do you see that makes you say that?

What do you think the designer and/or maker was trying to say through this object?
    —What do you see that makes you say that?

What do you think this object says about:
    —The time in which it was made and/or used?
    —The environment in which it was made and/or used?
    —The culture in which it was made and/or used?
    —What do you see that makes you say that?

Connecting with the Visitor at the Victoria and Albert Museum: Moving from Programme Design to Gallery Design*

Gail Durbin, Head of Gallery Education, Victoria and Albert Museum

The Victoria and Albert Museum, which was founded after the Great Exhibition in 1851, is the greatest decorative arts museum in the world. Like many other museums, the V&A offers education programmes carefully tuned to the needs of its audiences. We aim to be reflective practitioners, attempting to marry educational theory and practice.

Our family programmes provide an example of our methodology. The programmes are based on the understanding of the family as a learning unit with the following characteristics.[1]

- Families want to spend leisure time together on a worthwhile pursuit.
- They see the visit as a whole.
- They allow the child to drive the visit.
- They exhibit different behaviours according to the activity offered.
- The children learn through physical activity, experience and play.
- The adults want ideas and suggestions for activities or discussion with their children.
- The adults make up answers if they can't find them.

*To retain the original feel of the paper, the British spellings and names have been kept.

We therefore try to organise our programmes so that they encourage interaction between adult and child and provide plenty of support for the adult. The most concrete example of this is our "family trail," which comes in two parts—a trail for children and a leaflet for the accompanying adult that includes answers, further information, suggestions of questions to ask and ideas to follow up at home. Our best programmes succeed because they are very audience-focused and because we operate at that point where museum resources and audience need meet. How then do we translate the audience expertise that we have gained through running programmes into the development of galleries that also relate to the needs of those audiences?

The British Galleries Project:

At the V&A we are redisplaying our galleries of British art and design from 1500 to 1900. This is a five-year, £31 million lottery-funded project set up under the leadership of Christopher Wilk, the Chief Curator of the Furniture and Woodwork Department. The other members of the concept team are Sarah Medlam, Deputy Curator of the Furniture and Woodwork Department, and me. It was our job to set out the principles for the development of the gallery and its content.

The British Galleries take up ten percent of the V&A display space, cover 3,000 square metres, and extend over two floors. They have not been substantially redesigned for 50 years. This project has given us the opportunity to review the way we present our collections to the public.

Audiences:

We started by defining the audiences for the galleries. Our target audiences are:

- independent learners[2];
- families;
- school groups;
- Further and Higher Education groups[3];
- the local audience;
- ethnic minority groups[4];
- overseas visitors;
- specialists, amateur and professional.

This is a very high number of target audiences, but the decision was made because the galleries cover such a large proportion of the Museum's display space. If we were dealing with a single gallery, then it might have been appropriate to have a single primary audience but we felt we had to be inclusive. The decision caused some anxiety within the Museum. There was a fear that we would alienate our traditional audiences and some people imagined that one consequence would be eight different sets of labels.

In reality these audiences overlap. It is possible to be a specialist but to arrive as part of a family visit. The groups were chosen because the people in them have common learning needs and our intention was to identify the needs of each group, just as we do in planning programmes, and use the resulting lists as a means of checking whether our gallery plans catered to all our visitors.

We carried out a literature search to find what research added to our understanding of the needs of each of the groups, and we then tried to work out the implications for gallery design. Here the independent learner is given as an example.

Independent learners:[5]

- manage their own learning (they are not driven by a formal curriculum);
- are motivated by internal incentives and curiosity;
- draw on own experiences, cultural background and interests;
- are problem-centred (may, for example, wish to know how to dress the set for an amateur dramatic society production);
- are not restricted by conventional subject boundaries (so that the curatorial divisions, such as textiles and dress or ceramics and glass, will have little importance to an independent learner interested in gardening or bee-keeping);
- see themselves as part of a larger learning community that incorporates word of mouth and networks.

We learned that in designing galleries for these learners, museums should:

- concentrate on providing varied methods of interpretation and a choice of routes through the interpretation, rather than worry too much about details of content. By definition, it is not possible to predict the subject matter that will interest an independent learner;
- review museum practice. There is a conflict between the needs of independent learners and normal museum practice. The latter is expert-directed; that is, it creates dependence on the expert, takes no account of differences in prior knowledge and experience, and takes no account of interest that is for a practical purpose;
- include in the galleries connections with ideas and information elsewhere inside and outside the museum;
- make museum decision-making more transparent;
- give visitors the opportunity to take on the role of expert within the galleries;

- find ways for visitors to exchange information;
- provide study areas.

Learning style:

Apart from auditing our interpretation to check that each of the eight audiences is catered for, we have also tried to check that we are providing interpretation for a variety of learning styles.[6] At the moment the museum caters very well to analytical learners, presents some stimulus for common-sense learners but does little for experiential and imaginative learners except in the case of sophisticated museum-users who are able to make these leaps without the aid of interpretation.[7]

The concept of learning style came under attack at the Symposium from Philip Yenawine. As a learning theory, it was felt to be based on inadequate research and as an approach to visitors, it was thought to be reductive. Whilst recognising that learning style may have weakness as an educational theory, it acts as an extremely good model for an audit of the interpretative devices in a museum gallery. It may be desirable for all interpretative approaches to stimulate the full range of human learning behaviour, but in practice this is not always possible. It is evident that the majority of art museums limit their gallery interpretation to certain forms of thinking and learning—at the V&A there is little of a practical nature and no imaginative activities are currently built into gallery design. By using learning styles as a checklist, we plan to broaden the basis of our own interpretation.

Organisation of galleries:

We established the principle that interpretative devices would be placed next to the object being interpreted since the purpose of the interpretation was to encourage visitors to look at the object more carefully. Certain exceptions have been made. The messier activities will be placed in one of three activity rooms, there are rooms for major audio/visual presentations on each floor, and a study area on each floor will allow visitors to consult books and a computer database as well as pause for rest and reflection.

On content we decided that the galleries were to be organised chronologi-cally and there were to be four themes:

- Style
- Who led taste?
- Fashionable living
- What was new?

Three period teams were set up with one educator attached to each team.

Research:

Because this project is well funded, because the Heritage Lottery Fund is involved and because we want the project to act as a model, it has been possible to conduct extensive research. We started by surveying research done previously at the V&A. There was only one item lodged in the National Art Library at the V&A, and the Marketing Department had a run of Market and Opinion Research International (MORI) surveys conducted over several years. However, further enquiry tracked down a total of 63 pieces of work done in the V&A over the last ten years, many of which lurked in the back of people's filing cabinets.

The research programme consisted of:

- a commissioned summary of the last ten years of audience research at the V&A[8];
- a quantitative study commissioned at the outset to establish what people thought of the old British Galleries and how they behaved there[9];
- a study of how people used the first discovery area to be introduced into the V&A in the Silver Gallery[10];
- qualitative research on disability issues[11];
- qualitative research on the proposals for the galleries[12];
- formative research on our interpretative ideas. We are now starting to prototype some of our ideas. We have a temporary gallery, which displays some of the major objects while the galleries are built, and in this we have been testing ideas. We do this through observation and interview[13];
- further summative research once the galleries are open.

Key findings from the research:

1. Our audiences

Initial quantitative research[14] showed the percentages of people in the old galleries who identified themselves as belonging to our target groups.

Specialists—23 percent
Independent learners—62 percent[15]
Families—31 percent
Overseas visitors—44 percent[16]

The numbers in the four other groups (schools, students, the local community and ethnic minority groups) were too low to be significant.

Visitors to the old galleries do not reflect the social make-up of the population of Britain as a whole, as the following chart shows.

Social group[17]	British Galleries (per cent)	Great Britain (per cent)
AB	47	21
C1	40	27
C2	>9	23
DE	—	29
No answer	4	—
Base	252	

The findings also challenged assumptions made about our visitors by Museum staff who tend to think visitors share their understanding of the geography of the building and have a relatively sophisticated grasp of the organisation of displays. Research showed that 75 percent of visitors interviewed in the old British Galleries had no particular intention of visiting them and that, despite these galleries being organised chronologically, 4 out of 10 visitors said there was no particular organisation to the galleries. The findings also demonstrated the diversity of frequency of visiting. Whilst 56 percent of people were visiting the Museum for the first time, 13 percent had visited on at least ten other occasions.

But the most telling piece of information was the extraordinarily small amount of time most people spent in the old British Galleries. Fifty percent of visitors had left the lower floor galleries within 11 minutes (which is quite a challenge considering the size of these galleries). On the other hand 10 percent of visitors were still there after an hour, which provides further evidence of the diversity of the use of the Museum.

2. Gallery content

Work with focus groups representing our eight audiences teased out a mass of information about our visitors' feelings about the proposed content of the galleries. People were happy with the four themes and felt it was the Museum's job to choose these. They wanted dates as a means of orienting themselves. They felt we had omitted design and the creative process and the perspective of both rich and poor from our proposals. Interactives should be designed to help visitors see the objects more clearly. They should not impair the calm of the gallery. The "serene" atmosphere was liked and felt to be good for children as a contrast to other museums (and daily life).

We were concerned about how visitors would feel about the Style theme. How would they deal with the difficult vocabulary that a museum like ours cannot avoid: words like Baroque, Rococo, Gothic and Neo-Classicism?

A quiz showed that people had huge difficulty with style terms. Only the specialists were really secure. Other groups were able to orientate themselves chronologically via dress and architecture that were familiar from television and the movies (Jane Austen, *Blackadder* and *Mrs. Brown* were all mentioned). We will try to use dress and architecture as markers throughout the galleries.

What also came out, however, was a strong desire to know about style. The knowledge was thought valuable. It carried status.

> *Knowledge and confidence about style is tantamount to asserting you are a cultured (enlightened) person. There is a snob value to it, and class grievances are inextricably linked. People can be huffy and sensitive about being ignorant of style details. Other people pooh-pooh the whole area as being too pretentious to bother with. Almost everyone who can conceive of visiting the V&A wants to learn a bit about style: to leave with a little packet of knowledge that advances them in this fraught area.[18]*

If people were first helped with a historical and social context, then they felt they could move on to learn about style.

3. Text

Because of our desire to meet the needs of our eight target audiences we have spent time on thinking how to make the gallery text as accessible as possible. We considered Ekarving our text. This is a Swedish method, developed by Margareta Ekarv, of writing easy-to-read text. She sees museum text as a specialist form of writing. She emphasises simple language and rhythm. Sentences reflect natural phrase breaks and the printed text appears unusual in layout, with the varied line lengths of poetry. Those who liked it often commented on its clarity:

> *"I prefer the flow of it. It's easier and doesn't look as if you have to read too much. It's a bullet point format."*

The two groups who were most likely to find it useful were people whose first language was not English and highly educated people who, we speculate, may be more used to scanning text very quickly for content. On the whole, however, visitors to the V&A did not find the form a useful one. They were surprised and distracted by the layout:

> *"I dislike it. It detracts from the message. The rhythm is broken and I think 'Have I missed something? Why have they done this?' It's a bit trendy."*

This is a subject that would repay more research but we have decided, for now, to drop Ekarving for British Galleries text.

For object labels we experimented with four label formats. In one we tried offering the commentary first followed by all the museum information. A strong preference was expressed (59 from a sample of 106) for:

- Title and date and materials
- Production details
- Commentary
- Acquisition details

One reason for the popularity of this format was that picking out the date at the top made it easier for people to fit the object into their personal conception of a period in history. Secondly this format split the text up into four paragraphs rather than three which allowed skim-reading behaviours.

4. Encouraging people to participate

We want visitors to be actively involved in the galleries and to this end we have planned a series of drawing activities. Research shows that how these are presented is crucial to their success.

When we called an activity *Draw an acanthus leaf,* we found visitors were anxious about their own drawing skills because the instruction had made them focus on the outcome. They took longer to complete the activity and some asked for erasers and soft pencils. When we adjusted the activity and called it *Try an 18th century drawing book: find out what it was like to be an apprentice craftsperson 250 years ago,* their attitude changed. Visitors were more relaxed, completed the task, did not ask for soft pencils and made more empathetic, insightful comments. They were more focused on the process rather than the outcome and so appeared to learn more from the activity. Prototyping is allowing us to improve the effectiveness of our interpretative devices through minor changes such as these.

5. Potential areas for further research

When asked in the old galleries to rate learning on a scale of 1 (low) to 10 (high), a very uneven pattern emerged. People who gave answers of less than 5 were asked for a reason for their answer.

- 18 percent said they knew a lot already;
- 38 percent said they had walked through the galleries too quickly (which in itself is an implicit criticism of the displays);
- 44 percent said they had come to look at and enjoy the art and did not consider this a form of learning.

If we are interested in learning in museums, then we need to understand how people perceive their own learning in art museums and the vocabulary that they use to express that understanding.

6. Our own practice

Audience research has taught us much about how to work in the future:

Proposals should always be tested: In the *Telling Tales* series, which will focus on stories that we may no longer be familiar with illustrated on objects, two versions of the story of Aeneas' escape from Troy were recorded. The crackling sounds of fire and the creaking of the boat's timbers, added for dramatic effect, were not liked, possibly because they sounded like faults on the handset. As a result, we will be cautious with the use of sound effects on other audios in the series. Visitors confirmed that they did like the poetic language of the translation we used rather than a more updated version, and they appreciated the version that set the object in a personal context.

Proposals should be tested in the gallery not at a desk: We plan a number of *Object in Focus* videos showing aspects of objects that cannot normally be seen such as undersides or insides or, in one case, a washstand by William Burges with water flowing and the silver fish in the bowl flashing though the moving water as though it were swimming. Prototyping the video in the gallery taught us that although it may appear slow (it has sub-titles) when sitting in an office watching it, when placed in the gallery next to the object, it is not. Visitors were observed flicking back and forth between video and object, and around half of them found the video went a little too fast for them to keep up.

Audience research can be used to challenge institutional assumptions: There is a belief amongst many V&A staff that dressing up is an activity only for children. Observation disproves that. Of the 31 people observed trying on the replica corset and crinoline, 14 were adults. The range of time devoted to the activity was between 9 seconds and 7 minutes 30 seconds. It was a very successful activity and there was lots of smiling and chatter and comments such as: "Very good, I've only read about this." It attracted many passers-by, some of whom sat down to watch while deciding whether they were going to try the activity. It was seen as an important photo opportunity, and one visitor even went away to buy an instant camera to record the event.

Prototyping can be used to develop different kinds of activity more suited to different learning needs: Research on independent learning shows that for effective learning to take place, we need to change the balance of power in museum displays. Independent learners need to be given more credit for their own expertise and we are experimenting with ways of doing this. I am very interested in finding ways of putting the visitor into the role of expert.

In one activity we asked visitors to develop their own creative approaches to a painting of a man grasping the hind legs of a stag and share them with other visitors. The task was to write a mini-saga (a story of 50 words with a beginning, a middle and an end) about an object. These are two of the responses:

This man, after witnessing the miracle of dawn "awakening" the world, mistook his guardian stag as a means of escaping the wrath of the sun as it began its reign over all things living. So paralysed was he by the spectacle of a new day that he believed his only course of action was to clutch onto the stag and journey with it to a time and place beyond reproach of the celestial orb.

His wife asked him to bring home some meat for the table evening because they were expecting important guests. Unfortunately, being an accident-prone man he had lost his horse earlier that day through not watching where he was riding, and being knocked off his horse by a low branch. On returning home, on foot, because his horse had bolted (he had borrowed his brother-in-law's horse) he saw an opportunity that could not be missed....

In a display of commemorative objects we will ask people to tell us about any objects of commemoration that they possess and why those objects are significant to them. This was one response we received when we tested the activity.

I have two finely cut champagne glasses (from a set of 12) left from my grandmother's dowry. She married in 1911. With two world wars (this all happened in Germany) only two glasses survived. Even my grandmother died from bomb wounds in 1945. I look at the glasses and remember a lovely, gracious, impish lady with a love of life and for me, her first grandchild.

Elisabeth Mangerian, Fairport, New York, USA
(the 39th anniversary of my wedding) July 9, 1999

Visitor response activities are not traditional at the Victoria and Albert Museum and are risky activities to introduce. The prototyping process has convinced me they should have a place in our galleries. The quality of responses and the willingness of visitors to share with others significant emotional experiences have been both exciting and touching. It has added another dimension to our displays and confirmed that the experience that occurs in museum galleries is sparked where museum displays touch the concerns, experiences and preoccupations brought to the museum by the visitor.

Future web-based research:[19] Finally, there is an opportunity for people round the world to participate in our next iteration of audience research. Some of the computer material in our galleries will be Web-based.

We are working on the idea that visitors will be able to create their own personal album on a Web site. They can save information that interests them or designs they have created to that site, which can then be accessed from home, school or college. Alongside this, the Web will be used to create a visitor's book, some related discussion threads, and we plan a Web-based history project. Many of the period rooms in the galleries have been reconstructed through the use of inventories. We plan to invite visitors to join us in a project to assemble an archive. Visitors will be asked to tell us about the items they have bought over the last year for their front room. We anticipate that this will prove a valuable resource for the Museum in future years.

In this article I have attempted to show how an analysis of the needs of various audiences helps shape both programmes and gallery displays, how research has aided our work, and how the process of prototyping has allowed us to experiment with new methods of interpretation. But in the end it may not be educators who effect the greatest change in museums. It could be that the democratic and anarchic nature of the Web will be the factor that undermines the power of an institution like the V&A and places the visitor's voice firmly in the galleries in the role of expert.

ENDNOTES:

1. Much of our work on analysing different audience needs comes from David Anderson, *A report on museum education in the United Kingdom*, for the Department of National Heritage, in association with the DfEE (Department for Education and Employment), the Scottish Office, the Welsh Office and the Northern Ireland Office, first draft, unpublished, [1996].

2. Independent learners are those who learn from museums but are not governed by a formal curriculum. They are difficult to define precisely and could, on the most liberal definition, be any adult not part of a formal educational group who sets foot in a museum.

3. Further Education is generally vocational in character and available to students of 16+. Higher Education is generally academic in character and available to students of 18+.

4. In retrospect this was not a helpful grouping. The educational needs of an established community may be very different from one that is newly arrived. We would have been better off choosing to tackle separately access issues such as language or cultural difference.

5. Brookfield, S. (1986). *Understanding and facilitating adult learning*. San Francisco: Jossey-Bass.

6. Based on work by Kolb reiterated by B. McCarthy and B. Pitman-Gelles. (1998). "The 4MAT system: teaching to learning styles with right/left mode technique" Martin Sullivan et. al., eds., in *The Sourcebook*. Washington D.C.: American Association of Museums.

7. We have made some attempt to start researching the learning style of our audiences and how this influences their attitude to and enjoyment of the interpretation we have provided in our galleries. The results of that work will be published in December 1999 in *Museum Management and Curatorship* by Morna Hinton. "The Victoria and Albert Museum Silver Galleries II: Learning style and Interpretation Preference in the Discovery Area," *Museum Management and Curatorship*, Vol.17, No.3, due out mid-December 1999. A shorter version with key findings but not all the background theory, "'Learning Style and Interpretation Preference in the V&A Silver Gallery Discovery Area," will be published in *Museological Review*, Vol.6 in 2000.

8. Sara Selwood for the Policy Studies Institute, Survey of visitor research at the V&A, 1986-1996, March 1998.

9. Creative Research, Audience research for the British Galleries: quantitative research findings. Volumes 1 & 2, 29 March 1997.

10. Creative Research, Silver Gallery Discovery Area—Part 1: Introduction, summary of findings and recommendations. Part 2: Main findings of quantitative research. Part 3: Main findings of qualitative research, March 1998.

11. Managed by Colin Mulberg with Earnscliffe Davies as our consultant.

12. Fisher, S. (1998). "The British Galleries Project at the V&A: are people in tune with the new plans for interpretation?" *Qualitative research with visitors and non-visitors*, The Susie Fisher Group, August.

13. Managed by Morna Hinton with Paulette McManus as our researcher and consultant.

14. 252 people were interviewed. Of the 1,012 people approached 330 refused, 129 were rejected because they were either under 12 years of age or V&A staff, and 301 were excluded because there was no common language. This last figure indicates that there must be a considerable bias in much of our audience research.

15. Independent learners are difficult to research. For the purposes of this specific survey they were defined as anyone who said they had done any one of the following: planned to visit the British Galleries; belonged to a related club or society; expressed a professional or amateur interest; could specify something they had learnt from the galleries.

16. Other basic information: 49 percent of visitors arrived alone, 39 percent as a couple and 12 percent with three or more. 3 percent arrived with under 10 year olds, 7 percent with teenagers and 90 percent with adults or alone.

17. Definitions based on occupation of head of household. A: higher managerial, administrative or professional; B: Intermediate managerial, administrative or professional; C1: Supervisory clerical and junior managerial, administrative or professional; C2: Skilled manual worker; D: Semi-skilled or unskilled; E: Those at lowest level of subsistence, state pensioners, etc, with no other earnings.

18. Fisher, S. (1998). "The British Galleries Project at the V&A: are people in tune with the new plans for interpretation?" *Qualitative research with visitors and non-visitors*, The Susie Fisher Group, August, Chart 62.

19. The address of the V&A Web site is www.vam.ac.uk and we hope this project will be available there by March 2001.

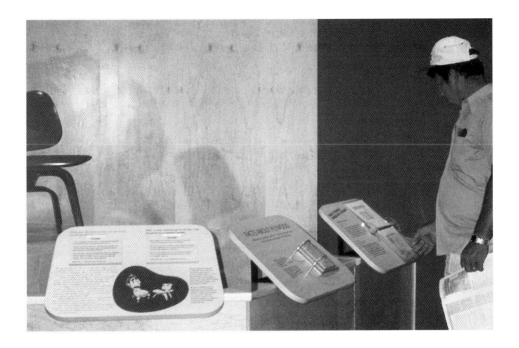

Funky and Fancy Furniture:
New Life for an Old Exhibit at Henry Ford Museum

Donna R. Braden, Experience Developer
Gretchen W. Overhiser, Experience Developer
Henry Ford Museum & Greenfield Village

Background:

Our work on the furniture exhibit at Henry Ford Museum began in 1996 when The Americana Foundation offered to either help us do something fresh with our extensive collection of furniture or help us sell it. Our old, tired exhibit had been on the Museum floor essentially unchanged for many years. The entrance was hard to find, the labels in the exhibit indicated only style and date, and visitors (when seen in the exhibit at all) were generally observed using the exhibit as a passageway from one place in the Museum to another. However there were some positive things about our collection that encouraged us to take up the offer to rethink our installation. Henry Ford Museum's furniture collection is considered one of the best in the country. It had been well documented during the 1980s by internal staff and outside experts who demonstrated enthusiasm for the quality and uniqueness of many of our pieces. We also felt that this collection had potential relevance to current museum audiences. This belief was supported by the Museum's market research, which told us that the furniture exhibit was very popular among our female visitors who constitute more than half of our total audience.

The charge to the exhibit team was to:

- provide the best fit with the Museum's mission;
- match visitor interests;
- find the people behind the objects;
- make the best use of our resources;
- provide a model for creating future new exhibits around the Museum's other extensive decorative arts collections.

The physical manifestation of our work was to create two (this later changed to three) new experimental exhibit components that would exist within the space of the larger exhibit. The actual structure of the exhibit was to remain substantially unchanged, but we were able to re-write labels, repaint and add some additional platforms. Because of storage considerations and staff time, we were also restricted in the number of objects that we were able to take off or put on exhibit.

Approach to Re-interpreting the Exhibit:

Our approach consisted of three major elements:

- Assessment of our collection using a worksheet we developed
- Research trips assessing other museums exhibits
- Evaluation—Baseline/Front-end/Formative

Throughout the 18-month process, our team organized a "learning in museums" discussion group and invited a larger group of Museum staff to attend our weekly get-togethers. At these learning lunches, we discussed applications of various readings to our own museum exhibits and programs. Topics ranged from learning styles, to how adolescents and families learn, to how fun fits into learning. These sessions both broadened the thinking of staff new to these ideas and deepened the knowledge of those already acquainted with them.

Assessment of Collections:

This element consisted of looking at every object in our collection and reviewing the documentation. The team then assessed mission fit as well as the people and social contexts behind each object. We also immersed ourselves in the published materials on furniture history and connoisseurship. In addition to identifying specific historical topics and/or stories that recurred, we also kept notes during our discussions about interesting questions, ideas and phrases that might develop into exhibit ideas later on.

Research Trips:

Team members undertook several trips to see what other museums had to offer and to test our ideas against those of other people who worked with similar collections. On each of these visits, we viewed exhibits and/or programs and talked with staff. After each trip, we compiled written reports, detailing what we saw and what our impressions were, along with related photographs and supplementary materials. Some of our many visits included the "Furniture City" exhibit at the Van Andel Museum in Grand Rapids, Michigan; the Winterthur Museum; the Toledo Museum of Art; the Maryland Historical Society; the DeWitt Wallace Gallery at Colonial Williamsburg; the Peabody Essex Museum; Historic Deerfield; the Heinz History Center in Pittsburgh, Pennsylvania; the Indianapolis Children's Museum; and the Strong Museum in Rochester, New York.

As a way of understanding how design, construction and market are interconnected in the furniture industry today, we talked to La-Z-Boy, Inc., headquartered in Monroe, Michigan, as well as staff and students at Kendall College of Art and Design in Grand Rapids, Michigan.

Evaluation—Questions and Results:

From the start of the project we had considered how we might utilize our great resource—visitors—to help create an exhibit that would be both relevant and engaging. This project represented the first time that an exhibit team at our institution had committed to using visitor studies to substantially help shape an exhibit. At the start of the project we did not have a cohesive overall plan for our evaluation. Being fairly new to using evaluation to shape an exhibit, we decided to start with what we thought of as a "baseline" evaluation so that we could learn a little about how people were using the old exhibit.[1] These baseline evaluations gave us a place to start thinking about how we might shape our overall evaluation plan. We decided that what would be most useful was to embark on a series of evaluations that could potentially help inform the shape the exhibit took—from the themes we emphasized to the way we wrote labels. Our evaluations were clearly intended to be very specific to the needs of this exhibit. They were usually very short-term, with data being gathered over a series of days for one or two weeks. Each evaluation had a very specific purpose and was developed by the lead evaluator with input from the entire team. The results of every evaluation were shared with the team and discussed. In the end, we reflected that nearly every aspect of the final exhibit plan was informed by our evaluations and contributed greatly to making this a successful exhibit.

Along with doing our own evaluations, we delved into research and evaluations undertaken by other institutions that had relevance to our work. Studies done by Randi Korn at Hillwood in Washington, D.C., The Denver Art Museum and Winterthur gave us ideas and insight far beyond what we would have been able to undertake on our own.

Re-interpretation and Installation:

The input from our collections assessment, research and visitor studies provided us with an extensive list of exhibit changes. In the end, our choices of what to do were so limitless and the decision-making was so difficult that it probably would have been easier to have planned a whole new exhibit!

1) Entrance

The new entrance or "gateway experience" arouses visitors' curiosity and expectations, and most important makes the exhibit easier to find. Our baseline evaluation informed us that all of the visitors who had been looking for the old exhibit found it very difficult to find. The two sides of the new entrance are curved, providing an inviting entry point to the rest of the exhibit. Six very enticing and visually distinctive pieces of furniture are highlighted here, displayed on appropriately textured platforms. Each piece is set in front of a lighted column that displays six words that visitors selected as best describing each piece of furniture.

2) A 1950s room setting

This new component, an immersive experience testing story-based and theatrical presentation techniques, was added. We chose to dramatically interpret a family's furniture "move" in progress in a 1950s living room. Work done at the Denver Art Museum suggested that pictures of room settings and room vignettes were popular with visitors because people like to imagine themselves as living in the space. A few older room vignettes at the Museum offered people the chance to imagine themselves in the space, but little opportunity for learning or relating to how they interacted with furniture in their own lives. The scenario of this room setting portrays a family in the process of updating the room with modern furniture and relegating the previous generation's old furniture to the attic or to the tag sale in the backyard. Several interactive elements enhance the story, including taped conversations of different family members about this move on period telephones, a decorating scrapbook in the form of a flipbook, a family photograph album and related postcards in the mailbox that visitors can peruse. The goal of this room setting is to encourage visitors to discover that the furniture that people acquire and cherish is a reflection of their individual values, aspirations and emotional needs.

3) Compare Two Chairs

This more straightforward, cognitively focused exhibit component presents two examples of furniture in which decoration and construction are interrelated. (Decoration and construction were the two most highly ranked topics when visitors were asked what interested them most about furniture.) For this component, we chose a side-by-side display of two very different-looking chairs made about

100 years apart—an 1850s rococo revival parlor chair and a 1946 lounge chair designed by Charles and Ray Eames. Our choice of chairs was inspired by the results of a photo sort where we asked people to look at photos of five chairs (a total of 20 photos were used to form a number of sets that were tested and cross-tested). Visitors were then asked to rank their favorite and least favorite of these chairs and tell us why they made their selections. The two chairs most frequently selected as favorites (and the chairs we decided to use in this exhibit component) both had strong red elements (upholstery and stain, respectively). Except for the similarity in color, these two chairs appear to be extremely different. But in fact both of them were made using a similar innovative plywood technique in their construction. Our goal was to communicate—through non-traditional labels and interactive elements—that although these two chairs appear quite different, they share some very similar characteristics. Our choice of labels reflects visitor interviews, which showed that people's knowledge about plywood tended to fall into two disparate categories—little to none or a highly technical level.

4) Family Activity Packs

We developed "Furniture Fun Packs," or portable learning kits, geared toward families with children ages 4 to 12. These packs—housed in canvas shoulder bags that can be checked out in the Museum's Hands-On Area—contain specific interactive materials that relate to four sections of the exhibit: kids' furniture, storage chests, comfortable seating and two plywood-constructed chairs that can be tried out. We developed these packs because we learned—through observation and through our readings—that to become really engaged in a museum exhibit like furniture, the family audience in particular needs highly involving activities. The goals of these packs are to provoke inquiry and learning, foster group interaction, help adults and children develop visual skills and encourage them to look at furniture in light of their own lives and experiences.

5) General Upgrades to the Rest of the Exhibit

We decided that it was crucial to improve the appearance of the rest of the existing furniture exhibit, despite our meager resources. Our first challenge was the organization of the furniture. As we restructured the entrance and considered the results of the visitor evaluations, we concluded that organizing the furniture according to chronology or style was an unappealing approach. We decided to re-group the furniture based upon primarily visual connections, often influenced by clues that visitors had given us about how they classified objects. These classifications were interesting to us, not least because when we first started to see patterns in the way that our visitors were classifying these objects, we were shocked! We were tempted to dismiss their alternative notions about how things should be grouped together as naïve and superficial. However, after much debate and discussion, we realized that if visitors were classifying things in a way that made sense to them, it provided us with an entry point to engaging them. Objects on display, therefore, are grouped together for such reasons that they all appear to be (or were perceived at a certain time in history to be) "comfortable"; show decorative painting; were used for storage; or have a specialized purpose. As visitors encounter these groupings, they are encouraged to actively explore the ways in which these objects are linked—both through their own observation and through accessible and involving new labels.

Conclusion:

Learning was certainly a key word for us in this project. We learned, of course, a lot about furniture. We also learned about presentation techniques, about the state of the museum field and the furniture industry, about the receptivity and opinions of visitors and about developing a process for a project that could serve as a template for planning future projects.

This was certainly not the most traditional way of planning and implementing an exhibit. There were definitely problems, particularly when it came time to make decisions about the specific exhibit elements. We think that the truly unique aspect of this project was its visitor focus from beginning to end. We did not start by choosing historical themes and then planning an exhibit around them. We started by observing how the subject of furniture engages our visitors, then tested our findings through exhibit approaches. Ultimately, engaging in the exhibit planning process this way dramatically changed the way we think about all of our exhibits and about visitors to our museum in general. As we begin to apply what we learned to future exhibits of all kinds—not just decorative arts exhibits—we think that current and future audiences to our museum will reap the benefits.

ENDNOTES:

1. What we termed "baseline" evaluation was actually summative evaluation done on an old exhibit, but since it did in fact enable us to establish a baseline from which to evaluate future changes to the exhibit, we titled it thus internally.

Evaluating *Baltimore Painted Furniture* at the Maryland Historical Society

Jeannine Disviscour, Associate Curator, Maryland Historical Society
Dale Jones, Senior Associate, Institute for Learning Innovation

In this paper, Dale Jones and I will discuss the methodology, evaluation, insights and implications of the Maryland Historical Society's test exhibition *Baltimore Painted Furniture*, which opened on June 4, 1998. I will document the project background, overview and goals; Dale will detail the evaluation process and results of Phase I and the responses to Phase II of the project. I will then describe the changes made in the *Baltimore Painted Furniture* reinstallation, and will conclude with implications for future MHS exhibitions.

Project Background, Overview and Goals

The *Baltimore Painted Furniture* exhibition and evaluation project was a successful endeavor with results that are highly important to the Maryland Historical Society (the Museum). This evaluation was the first major step the Museum has taken to obtain our public's opinion on an exhibition and act on it in a comprehensive way. In earlier exhibitions the Museum:

- Solicited opinions from our visitors in "Comment Books";
- Asked visitors to add important events in their lives to local and national "Time Lines";
- Prompted our visitors to respond to topical questions.

Never before have we planned to comprehensively use the resulting information for future installations or change an exhibition in response to these comments. What compelled this change? First, an institution-wide conceptual shift prompted by our director Dennis Fiori's commitment that the MHS teach Maryland history in a meaningful way that is family-friendly and accessible to a broad audience. The MHS looks to implement these goals through permanent and temporary exhibitions, educational programs and publications. The second factor that affected this change was funding. In December 1996, the MHS received a generous grant from the Dorothy Wagner Wallace Charitable Trust for the creation of a state-of-the-art gallery dedicated to the exhibition of furniture made and used in Maryland. The curatorial staff decided to use a portion of the funding to investigate how to best use our furniture collection to teach Maryland history. To take advantage of our timing and to get the most relevant data possible, we hired an outside evaluator, the Institute for Learning Innovation, to help us access this issue.

From its inception in 1844, the MHS has used its collections to serve its community through exhibitions, publications and a variety of programs. Museum collections now number over 250,000 objects. Furniture, in particular, has been an important component of this constellation of material and is especially suited to an exhibition that can tell and illustrate aspects of Maryland history. This nationally renowned collection includes 1,200 pieces of furniture made or used in Maryland in the 18th, 19th and 20th centuries.

The MHS collection is strong in neo-classical furniture and seating furniture from the late 18th to late 19th century, particularly Baltimore painted furniture. Late 20th-century collecting has focused on adding pieces from the Eastern Shore and Western Maryland as well as pieces that are relevant to a broader community and constituency. Recent acquisitions include a set of three painted chairs from Baltimore that were purchased in the early 19th century by recently-freed members of the Cummings family, who later became prominent in Baltimore's political and intellectual community.

The size and breadth of the overall MHS furniture collection places it among the most important regional collections of American furniture. The furniture collection provides an important overview of mid-Atlantic furniture production and patronage critical to the understanding of life in this part of the country. Very little of this tremendous collection, about eight percent, is actually on display and interpreted to the public. The interpretation of those objects on display, while interesting to furniture scholars, is about 15 years old and not particularly engaging to the diverse audience we now want to reach.

From the outset we knew that we would open the Dorothy Wagner Wallace Furniture Gallery with Baltimore painted furniture. The reasons were many: the MHS collection is particularly strong in these objects; the production of this product tells an important local, national and international story; the information and objects could be accommodated in the 400-square-foot gallery; and the subject was of specific interest to our funder. The initial exhibition team consisted of Jeannine Disviscour as project director and other staff curators, registrars and educators. The team began by interviewing every member of the MHS staff to identify how they envisioned the test gallery and the furniture gallery in general. The team felt strongly that the entire staff needed to be consulted to share their perspective and to feel connected to this initiative. Additionally, the needs of our core audience, that in the past were interested primarily in furniture style and design, were kept in mind.

The resulting plan of action was broad but significant: that we present the furniture with its historic context—that we not simply present rows of furniture with accession numbers (in a traditional study-storage format). After this initial phase of information gathering I added outside consultants (furniture experts), the exhibition designer (Charles Davidson of The PRD Group) and an outside evaluator (Dana Holland and, later, Dale Jones from the Institute for Learning Innovation) to the exhibition team. The full team worked together and identified the following exhibition goals:

- To teach Maryland history with furniture;
- To create a contextual, interactive and experimental presentation of the subject, which would allow a fresh discussion of furniture;
- To provide our visitors with the opportunity to see more furniture made or used in Maryland (get more furniture out of storage);
- To incorporate a discussion of aesthetic issues and style (to provide expected information for our traditional audience);
- To include the stories of those who made and used Baltimore painted furniture;
- To investigate how the pieces functioned within a larger context.

To reach these goals the exhibition designer laid out the exhibition so that the furniture was presented in three settings which focus on the different ways one can look at painted furniture: how it was made and sold, its design sources, and how it functioned in the home. The entire team made recommendations about the exhibition content, hands-on activities, object labels, design, titles, what to evaluate and how to perform this evaluation. The resulting Phase I of the exhibition consisted of an introduction, three interpretive sections and a comment area.

Phase I Installation

Introduction:

Located in the center of the exhibition space, this section placed the entire subject within the context of local, national and international history. This placement was deliberate. Institute for Learning Innovation researchers have found that visitors tend to skip introductions to exhibitions when the introductions are lengthy and located at the beginning of exhibitions.[1] Institute researchers recommend de-centralized introductions. By using this approach, we felt the visitor would be more likely to read or reference the information.

"Baltimore: A Center for Buying and Selling Furniture"

In this section visitors learn how painted furniture was made and sold. Hands-on activities include:

- A rail panel showing different woods used in making painted furniture;
- An opportunity to re-create the actions of a craftsman who turned chair legs;
- A coloring activity exploring colors used in the 19th century and today;
- And a presentation of the techniques used for applying painted decoration to furniture and the scientific methods used for discerning this information.

"Baltimore Painted Furniture: The Source of Its Style"

Here visitors learn about design sources. Hands-on activities in this section include:

- An activity that allows visitors to decorate a chair and table using large puzzle pieces;
- A lift-the-flap activity where visitors are invited to select one of four different chairs to experience the choices a buyer had when purchasing a chair in the early 1800s;
- And another lift-the-flap activity that invites visitors to look for classical designs in other objects in our collection.

"At Home with Baltimore Painted Furniture"

Featured here, in an elegant parlor setting, is an important suite of furniture, including an elegant sofa, window bench and pier table purchased by wealthy shipping merchant and investment banker Alexander Brown from John and Hugh Finlay around 1815. Paintings of Marylanders with Baltimore painted furniture and a discussion of how these furnishings functioned in the home round out this section. Hands-on activities include:

- A flip book with pages from Alexander Brown's account book, which allows visitors to view how Brown made his money;
- A flip book of James Wilson's 1851 household inventory;
- And a short audio segment with Rosalie Stier Calvert's comments about furnishings at "Riversdale."

The Comment Area is a dedicated space that provides visitors with the opportunity to sit and fill out our survey forms.

At the exhibition opening, on June 4, 1998, we began the formal evaluation process.

Phase I Evaluation

Overview:

The Institute for Learning Innovation (Institute), an Annapolis, Maryland-based non-profit research and evaluation organization, designed and implemented a formative evaluation, in collaboration with the MHS, to study:

- How visitors used the gallery;
- What sections of the exhibit visitors liked most;
- What visitors thought about the text and hands-on areas;
- What visitors learned, and what changes they might recommend.

Three methodologies were designed to gather visitors' interactions with, and impressions of, the Painted Furniture Gallery: a self-reported questionnaire, visitor tracking and visitor interviews.

Questionnaires were placed in the exhibit and filled out voluntarily by visitors. A total of 107 visitors elected to participate in this self-reported gallery evaluation. The questionnaire asked visitors questions to elicit the following information:

- Which sections of the exhibit are most interesting?
- Which "Please Touch" parts were used and liked?
- What three things did visitors learn?
- How much of the information did visitors read?
- Was the description and information interesting, understandable and sufficient?
- What was the main idea?
- What else would visitors like to know?
- What changes would visitors make?

The Institute also designed a tracking instrument to assess visitor movement throughout the gallery, interest/engagement with particular exhibit elements, and time spent in the gallery. Institute researchers and MHS staff then tracked 17 visitors through the gallery over the summer and fall of 1998.

Finally, the Institute developed questions to guide semi-structured interviews with visitors. The interview guide questions included:

- Generally, what did you think of the exhibit (or area/room you just walked through)?
- What did you find most interesting?
- What was your sense of the main idea (or theme) of the exhibit?
- The exhibit has three areas. Did that stand out for you? (i.e., Did they recognize spatial/intellectual organization of the space?)
- What suggestions do you have for how we could make the exhibit better?

Institute staff interviewed six visitors following their visit to the gallery. The size of this sample was limited by low visitation to the MHS and to this gallery during the summer.

The Institute then coded, entered, analyzed and interpreted the data, compiled through all three methodologies.

Highlights of Results:

Who Visited: Visitors who self-selected to complete questionnaires (n=107) were a mix of visitors in families (45 percent) and all adult groups (44 percent). Almost one quarter (24 percent) were members. Almost half of these visitors (46 percent) had visited the Maryland Historical Society (MHS) previously.[2]

The majority of the visitors resided either in Baltimore (35 percent) or elsewhere in Maryland (37 percent). The rest of the visitors (28 percent) were visiting the gallery from elsewhere in the United States. Substantially more women/girls (74 percent) than men/boys (26 percent) completed a questionnaire. Most of those completing questionnaires were adults aged 31-55 (40 percent), and many were children less than 12 years old (21 percent) or teenagers (8.5 percent). The remainders were equally distributed among those in the 19–30 and over-55 age groups.

Tracking: Visitors spent anywhere from 25 seconds to 15 minutes in the gallery. Almost one half (47 percent) spent from 5 to 15 minutes with 35 percent spending 2 minutes or less and the remaining 18 percent spending 3 to 4 minutes. Forty-four percent of visitors attended most to *The Source of Its Style*, while 25 percent attended most to *At Home*.

Both adults and children appeared to use the rail panels more than the text panels, and there was some indication that the text panels that included graphics and/or photo reproductions were used more frequently than those containing text only.

"Please Touch" Results: The majority of visitors used at least one of the "Please Touch" components. Only eight visitors (7 percent) did not indicate using even one. Most used were "Choose a Chair" (70 percent) and "Try Your Eye at Design" (69 percent). Least used was "Color the Past" (51 percent). Components liked most are shown below in Table 1:

Please Touch components liked most:		
Try Your Eye at Design	42.9%	24
Color the Past	32.1%	18
Choose a Chair	25.0%	14
Turn a Chair Leg	23.2%	13
Rosalie Stier Calvert's Audio Comments	23.2%	13
Search for the Same Designs	21.4%	12
Totals	*	*
Replies		56

Note: Multiple answers can total over 100%.

Table 1: Interactives Visitors Liked Most in Phase I

What Visitors Learned: In responding to the questionnaire, most visitors (75 percent) readily indicated what they had learned and found particularly interesting in the exhibition. Nearly one-half (44 percent) of the visitors described learning about the variety of painted furniture, including varieties of styles, colors, woods used, types of furniture, etc. Over a quarter of the visitors (28 percent) described the relative costs of the furniture, while another 29 percent mentioned learning something about the process of production. Consistent with interview results, one quarter (25 percent) of the visitors specifically mentioned learning that Baltimore was a center for painted furniture.

Visitors' Observations on Text: While half of the visitors completing questionnaires indicated reading "most or nearly all" of the text (50 percent), observational findings and interviews indicated more modest use of the text. Almost all of these visitors (95 percent) reported that the descriptions were easy to understand. Most of these visitors (67 percent) thought that the descriptions were "just right." However, a quarter of the visitors (25 percent) claimed that they "wanted to know more."

Although most of those who read text found it interesting (98 percent) and easy to understand (95 percent), there were some visitors who felt the "verbiage" was prohibitively dense. In fact, 8 percent indicated that the descriptions were "too wordy." In an interview a self-described "reader" was worried that, "[the exhibition] was good because we did read, but if you don't read you might not get much out of it."

There was also some indication that visitors did not appreciate the overall spatial and conceptual organization of the exhibition. Several visitors commented that they did not understand that the exhibition was organized into three areas until they either completed a questionnaire or talked with a researcher. One visitor described being drawn to concept areas by objects rather than labels or text:

> *"When someone comes in, I go to certain area. I go to a piece that hits me [i.e., catches my eye]. There's a lot of information in here. My eye wants to see highlights, make it more obvious what is what, so people know. I see the organization now that you say so, but there is so much verbiage that it gets lost."*

Recommendations for Gallery Development:

Based on the analysis of the data from interviews, tracking and questionnaires, as well as on the experience of Institute researchers, the Institute made the following recommendations for changes to the Gallery for Phase II of the exhibit.

- Overtly label areas and exhibition items.
- Experiment with less block text by using bullet points and set important text in bold, employing more enticing topical labeling of text, and overtly connecting the text to objects on display. Text can be used as a graphic that guides visitors' eyes to information of interest.
- Themes relating to design and details about the furniture itself appear to be conveyed more so than themes about the process of production. In addition there was some indication that visitors did not fully appreciate themes relating to the use of painted furniture; specifically, several visitors did not seem to understand that the *At Home* section was a period room setting. It might be worthwhile to consider how to better convey exhibition themes that were seldom mentioned by visitors.
- Consider placing main ideas on rail panels in addition to placing them on the text panels.
- Consider creating an "advance organizer" panel (perhaps on the rail) that tells visitors what the main themes of the exhibit are.
- Consider adding more hands-on sections. Visitors liked them. If one or two were added to the *At Home* section, it might help to increase visitor interest in that section.

Phase II Installation

Following the Institute's recommendations, some specific visitor comments and curatorial concerns, the exhibition team approved and made the following changes to *Baltimore Painted Furniture* over the summer of 1999.

- The introductory area was rearranged to make it more visible and provide an "advance organizer" to tell the visitor the main themes of the exhibition.
- A dramatic signature object was hung in the introduction area to draw attention to the reformatted information.
- The introductory Baltimore/Maryland history information was moved to a rail panel.
- Each of the three sections of the exhibition was boldly labeled with a maroon and yellow title panel.
- The *At Home* section was altered to look more like a lived-in parlor: walls were wallpapered and more paintings and accessories were added.
- A large rail panel was removed to allow better views of the furniture in the *At Home* section.
- An *Arrange the Furniture* interactive was added to replace the James Wilson inventory flip book that was too hard to read and, while used, not very popular.
- The audio was taped with good sound equipment and we provided an audio transcription.
- The black and white photographs in *Choose A Chair* and *Search for the Same Designs* were replaced with color images.
- The *Turning* interactive was reworked to clarify the turning process.
- The visitor seating in the exhibition comment area was changed from contemporary stools to reproduction painted furniture to give visitors the opportunity to sit on a piece of painted furniture.
- And lastly we added life-size figures with a placard announcing the exhibition outside each door to lure visitors into the show and clarify that they were entering a special exhibition.

The revised exhibition opened to the public on July 1, 1999, and survey, tracking and interview data were collected until November 2, 1999.

Phase II Evaluation

Based on tracking of visitors, self-reported questionnaires and visitor interviews, Institute researchers found that changes made to the Gallery appeared to affect visitor experience mainly in the *At Home* section of the exhibition in terms of time spent in the space, interest in the space and use of the new interactive *Arrange the Furniture*.

Phase II Methodology:

The methodologies for Phase II remained consistent with Phase I: tracking, self-reported questionnaires and visitor interviews. Instruments were slightly revised in order to address the changes to the exhibition. In order to gauge visitor reaction to text panels, a question was added to the interview survey, which specifically addressed bulleted text and rail panels. Sample sizes for each methodology of Phase II were as follows: tracking: n=21; self-reported questionnaires: n=32; and interviews: n=8.

Results of Changes Made to the Painted Furniture Gallery:

While the majority of the Phase II data stayed consistent with Phase I data, there is evidence to indicate that the changes made to the *At Home* section and the changes made to text may have improved the visitors' experience. With the exception of visitor reaction to the *At Home* section, the Phase II study found little change in visitor behavior and reaction to the Painted Furniture Gallery. Data from both phases indicated that visitors enjoyed the exhibition and particularly liked the "Please Touch" components in the exhibition. In the following analyses, it should be kept in mind that the sample from Phase II was small, and interpretations of results outlined below, while indicating encouraging trends, should be done with caution.

Description of Phase II Visitor Sample:

Twenty-one visitors were tracked through the exhibition for Phase II. Of that group, 62 percent (n=13) were female and 38 percent (n=8) were male. One half (n=10) were lone adults, 40 percent (n=8) were in adult groups, and 10 percent (n=2) were in families.

Thirty-one people responded to the self-selected questionnaire, of which 89 percent (n=24) were female and 17 percent (n=5) were male. Sixty-two percent (n=18) were in family groups, 17 percent (n=5) in all adult groups, 19 percent (n=4) alone, and 7 percent (n=2) in tour groups. Ages of the sample were as follows:

20 percent (n=6)   less than 12 years
13 percent (n=4)   13–18 years
10 percent (n=3)   19–30 years
43 percent (n=13) 31–55 years
13 percent (n=4)   56 years or older

Sixteen percent (n=6) were from Baltimore, 53 percent (n=16) from Maryland, and 27 percent (n=8) were from elsewhere in the United States. Sixty-one percent (n=19) had never been to the MHS, while 38 percent (n=12) had visited before.

Based on the tracking data, visitors appeared to have spent more time in the *At Home* area in Phase II than they did in Phase I. In Phase I, 25 percent (n=4) spent the most time in the *At Home* area; in Phase II, 40 percent (n=8) spent most time in the *At Home* area. Likewise, when the areas that visitors spent the least time in were compared, in Phase I, 36 percent (n=5) spent the least time in *At Home*, but in Phase II, only 8 percent (n=1) spent the least time in *At Home*.

Likewise, visitors' usage (a subjective assessment by researchers of visitors' engagement with a section of the exhibition) increased in Phase II. Usage of the *At Home* area was compared in Phase I and Phase II using a scale of 1 to 5, with 1 being low usage and 5 being high usage. Fifty-one percent (n=8) of visitors in Phase I were tracked as having relatively high usage (rated 3 to 5) in the *At Home* area. This number increased in Phase II with 84 percent (n=15) of visitors using the *At Home* area with a high ranking of 3 to 5.

In addition to the tracking data, self-reported questionnaires also indicated a more favorable response to *At Home* in Phase II. While 66 percent (n=61) of Phase I visitors ranked the *At Home* area with "moderately high" to "high" interest level, 86 percent (n=19) of visitors in Phase II ranked *At Home* with "moderately high" to "high" interest level.

The new hands-on component of the *At Home* section, *Arrange the Furniture*, was also popular among visitors. *Arrange the Furniture* was ranked highest most often (37 percent, n=7) among visitors' favorite "Please Touch" components in the Phase II questionnaire. Based upon her interaction with *Arrange the Furniture*, one woman, in the 36-to-55-year-old age range, had an illuminating experience about how furniture was placed in a room. In describing the activity she stated, "It brought out in a very hands-on way how much furniture was normally in a room. I had no idea it was that crowded. It was different than reading a list…actually seeing a space and seeing the furniture and how it would work."

The activity *Rosalie Stier Calvert's Audio Comments*, which was also upgraded with a better recording and a transcript, also seemed to be more popular in Phase II, with 32 percent (n=6) of visitors preferring it and earning a second-most popular ranking. In Phase I, it was ranked second from the bottom in popularity with 23 percent (n=13).

Text Format:

Based on the recommendations in Phase I, some changes were made to the exhibition text. Specifically, some of the paragraph panels were changed to bulleted text, and based on curators' recommendations, some black and white photographs on labels were changed to color.

Overall, visitors' responses to text panels were very favorable in both Phases. Additional insights about the text panels can be gleaned from the interviews conducted during Phase II. Visitors were asked if they preferred rail text or wall text and if they preferred the bulleted format or the paragraph format. While the sample size for these interviews is very small, it should be noted that six of the eight visitors preferred rail panels to the text panels. One woman, aged 36 to 55 years, said, "I preferred it lower because I'm not very tall. If I had bifocals I would have to crane my neck back to read it."

Visitors also seemed to like the bullet format for text. Of the six responses, three visitors preferred bullets, two liked a variety of both formats (bulleted text and paragraphs), and one visitor had no preference. One senior male said, "Both have their advantages. Depends on how curious you are and if you really want to read all of that or if you are more like me coming in because I was in the historical society anyway and just came for a quick visit."

What Visitors Learned:

Visitors were asked in the self-reported questionnaire to write down three things they learned in the exhibition. Even though visitors' answers varied greatly it was clear that when data for both Phases were combined, visitors were able to note information about the main topics of the exhibition with some common categories emerging. Some of the most common answers included 43 percent (n=45) of visitors mentioning that they learned about the variety of painted furniture including styles, colors and wood; and 36 percent (n=38) of visitors commenting on different processes of production. For example, one young girl under 12 said, "I learned about making legs for furniture and caning chairs." It should also be noted that 24 percent (n=25) of visitors mentioned they learned that Baltimore was the center of painted furniture.

Data collected during Phase I indicated that many visitors were unable to articulate clearly the main themes or sections of the exhibition. To help improve their understanding, the introduction area was rearranged to include a larger text panel and a clear advanced organizer with bulleted text for the exhibition. In addition, a large text panel with a section heading was added to each section.

In order to determine if visitors were able to grasp these points, interviewees were asked two questions: 1) "If a friend asked you to state the main idea of this exhibition, what would you say?" and 2) "There are three sections to this exhibition. Did you notice that? What are they?" Only two of the eight visitors specifically stated that "Baltimore was the center for painted furniture." Two visitors mentioned painted furniture or the history of painted furniture. None of the eight interviewees could explain the three sections of the exhibition.

With only eight interviews, it is difficult to come to any definitive conclusions; however, it appears that visitor understanding of main ideas and sections did not change between Phase I and Phase II. One mitigating factor in visitors' identification of the separate sections may have been that the section headings, while brightly colored, were placed too high. Beverly Serrell noted in *Exhibit Labels: An Interpretive Approach* that visitors often do not see labels that are higher than six or seven feet above the floor.[3]

Another reason that visitors may not have been able to articulate themes is based on their agenda, or their reasons for coming to the Museum. Visitors come to museums for a variety of reasons, with leisure activity being one of their main motivators for attendance. Since they are visiting as part of a leisure activity, it is not unusual for visitors to have difficulty identifying the main idea and themes of an exhibition. In a study by the Institute for Learning Innovation at the National Museum of African Art, researchers discovered that visitors did not even realize that they had left the Arthur M. Sackler Gallery and gone into the National Museum of African Art through an underground tunnel.[4] To ask them also to identify the main sections of an exhibition when they were not even aware they were in a different museum would have been futile.

It is important to note that the visitors' inability to articulate the three exhibition sections should not undermine the importance of providing clarity and organization for visitors throughout the exhibition. Even though visitors cannot articulate the main themes does not mean that the structure and physical space have no effect on visitor understanding of the content being presented and of the visitor experience. In addition, providing such clarity and organization is of tremendous importance to staff creating the exhibition and complementary materials and programs.

Recommendations

Overall the positive visitor feedback indicated that the general approach to the Gallery could be a good model for developing future galleries. Based on data from Phase I and II, the Institute made the following recommendations:

1. Use advance organizers to assist visitors' understanding of main ideas and themes. Advance organizers function much like a table of contents in a book and provide visitors with a quick overview of what to expect in the exhibition. Beverly Serrell notes in *Exhibit Labels: An Interpretive Approach* that, "When visitors have good conceptual and spatial orientation in exhibitions, they are more likely to spend more time and learn more."[5] Advance organizers help provide that conceptual organization. Ideally they should be located where they can be easily seen and read as a visitor enters a gallery. For Phase II, the MHS did include advance organizers linked to an object (a painted chair), but because of space limitations MHS staff had to place the advance organizers within the exhibition in the middle of the wall opposite where visitors entered. Institute researchers were not able to determine whether the inclusion of the advance organizers in the Gallery had an effect on the visitor experience or not.

2. Clearly label or identify major exhibition areas. Visitors were unable to identify the three main content areas in Phase I. For Phase II, MHS staff attempted to identify the three areas more clearly by including a large label in striking color above each section and by clearly delineating the *At Home* section as described earlier. Visitors did spend more time with the *At Home* section but were still unable to identify the three main areas. One possible reason may have been that the labels were positioned too high for visitors to see easily, as mentioned earlier.

A more likely reason, as discussed earlier, may be that as museum staff, our expectations that visitors know and understand the main idea and themes may be the wrong expectations. Visitors come to museums for a variety of reasons, of which leisure activity is high on the list. Museum staff should still make every effort to maintain clear organization of the exhibition, but perhaps should not necessarily expect visitors to be able to recall explicitly the main themes and ideas of an exhibition.

3. Consider using bulleted text and bold important text information. Many visitors seemed to like getting their information "at a glance." While some visitors also liked the depth of information provided in paragraph panels, having some bulleted text helps visitors to understand important points quickly and easily. It is important to have a variety of options for visitors.

4. Continue to incorporate hands-on interactives within the exhibitions. The interactives allowed visitors to become involved with the exhibition, and many visitors commented on the appeal of the "Please Touch" activities. The changes made to the *At Home* section in adding *Arrange the Furniture* and in upgrading the *Rosalie Stier Calvert* audio appeared to lead to greater use, interest and time spent by visitors in that space and in some instances led to insights or "ah-ha" moments. As Serrell comments in *Exhibit Labels*, "Adults who read labels and those who use interactives are not two separate audiences."[6] The inclusion of interactive components should be considered in future exhibitions.

5. Consider placing main ideas on rail panels in addition to placing them on the text panels on walls. While the sample size of visitors interviewed was small, it appeared that most visitors preferred rail text because it was easier to

read and closer to the objects. When given the choice, rail panels should probably be considered in addition to, or instead of, wall text.

In this two-part study, the MHS has made inroads into understanding visitors'
experiences in an exhibition. By incorporating findings from the first phase of the
evaluation, the MHS has shown a desire to make its exhibitions more visitor-
friendly and more accessible to the public. The Society should be commended for
its efforts.

Future Implications

The data gathered over the entire course of the project has led to exciting
conclusions, some expected, others unexpected. The Maryland Historical
Society plans to incorporate the following recommendations in the design and
interpretation of future permanent and temporary exhibitions at the Museum.

1. We clearly recognize the importance of listening to our visitors and giving
them the opportunity to comment. The comments obtained in all three formats
provided valuable insights that helped us to better communicate our story of
Baltimore Painted Furniture. Visitor comments to the exhibition reinstallation
strongly demonstrate this. The MHS is now more committed than ever to
understanding its audience, and as of late summer 1999, has placed a permanent
comment box near our entrance to solicit responses to specific questions and to
capture more general responses. Our Visitor Services Committee, an interde-
partmental team, will respond to these comments.

2. To understand the limitations of thematic groupings. The visitors to
Baltimore Painted Furniture did not comprehend the three different thematic
groupings of furniture in the installation. Yet, they did understand the concepts
that each section laid out. Therefore, while thematic groupings are important as
a means for grouping and presenting material for curators and exhibition
designers, section content should be clearly included in the text.

3. Provide interpretive text in multiple levels: both physically and intellectually. The different levels provide variety and allow the text to avoid monotony.
Provide advance organizers where appropriate, and begin a large body of text
with the main idea in bold.[7] Additionally, do not shy away from providing
in-depth information when appropriate. Despite the large volume of information
to read in this exhibition, no one complained that there was too much text; on
the contrary, a few visitors requested more text or a book on the exhibition. The
level of interest in the large volume of text surprised us. Part of this response
may be due to the self-selecting nature of the responses to this survey. Most of
the visitors uninterested in this subject did not come into the gallery to view
the exhibition, nor did they take the time to respond to a survey. Those who did
respond were interested in Maryland history and furniture and wanted to learn more.

4. On a quite practical level, provide text where visitors can see it. It is likely that the rail panels were used more often because they were the closest to the viewer.

5. Use rail panels to convey the most important information. The rail panels' rich combination of interpretive text, interactive elements, and object labels along with their location made them the most popular vehicle for conveying information. For future furniture installations I would design a less obtrusive rail panel and provide more room between the rail panel and the objects on display. (We did get complaints that our yellow wooden rails were clunky and that they obscured objects directly behind them.) This will allow clearer viewing of the objects and provide better security.

6. Present the subject—whether it's furniture, silver, glass or paintings—in the context of Maryland history. Initially we conceived of the Maryland Furniture installation as primarily a "study-storage" facility: a line-up of furniture with little context. Given our mandate to teach history with our collections, we changed this approach to allow for interpretation and flexibility. My hope is that when we reinstall all our furniture, we will be able to put much more on display by varying the presentation's rhythm. We hope to employ the exhibition methods described in this study—such as vignettes and thematic groupings of objects interpreted in-depth—and combine them with groupings of related objects presented with less information that support the theme.

7. Provide visitors with the familiar—in this exhibition's case it was a solid section on style—and use nearby spaces to introduce new ways of looking. New interpretations on furniture production and function were adjacent to the section on style.

8. Incorporate hands-on activities within the body of the exhibition. Do not segregate them into a separate space in the installation or a separate room in the museum. This methodology is particularly effective for building a family audience. The various activities in *Baltimore Painted Furniture* drew both adults and children to all sections of the exhibition and supported and illuminated many aspects of the interpretation. Interestingly, in some cases children were occupied in various activities (*Color the Past, Try Your Eye at Design, Arrange a Room*) while their parents viewed the exhibition. Adults also often did the activities, either alone or with children, providing an opening for dialogue reinforcing knowledge on the subject of Baltimore painted furniture and Maryland history.

9. Continue to use our collection, as much as possible, to tell the story of Maryland's history. The historical narrative needs to be determined independently of collection objects. However, we need to allow the objects to tell personal stories and build upon these to illuminate national trends. After visitors have found the Maryland Historical Society and seen its collection, almost universally they are

impressed with its breadth and quality. The MHS's tremendous collection of objects and library material and our attempts to integrate them make us unique and is a draw in itself.

10. Production quality matters. The increased interest in the audio seen in Phase II was directly related to its improved quality. I initially tried to produce the audio for free. I used a Belgian speech teacher (Rosalie Stier Calvert was from Belgium) and poor taping equipment. For Phase II, I hired an actress and contracted with a sound person with high-quality equipment to record her. The difference in quality was tremendous although the equipment used to convey the audio in the exhibition remained the same. The higher interest in the Phase II vignette is another example of the value of production quality. The wallpaper, additional curtain, paintings and numerous personal items that were added provided the spark of life that was missing in Phase I. Again, these changes were an additional expense but provided the viewer with a more fulsome example of living with painted furniture.

11. Lastly, I want to emphasize the importance of a strong research foundation for all aspects of a project such as this, especially for producing meaningful and enlightening interactive elements. I used research completed by Gregory Weidman in *Furniture in Maryland* and *Classical Maryland* and performed additional research with information from Museum of Early Decorative Arts, the MHS, and other sources.[8] The team, with its broad range of expertise from American and European furniture to educational methodology, was an invaluable resource in boiling the information down into manageable bites, engaging titles in addition to interesting and fun hands-on activities. We trusted ourselves to provide the content, to be the experts and then to ask our visitors for their thoughts.

The Museum's strong furniture collection, track record of exhibiting furniture and the work of our former furniture curator built a strong and committed audience for this subject. As a result, we knew that we would have visitors to the exhibition and we would have a pool of responses. Our respondents, however, went beyond MHS members. Over half of those who responded to the survey were new to the MHS, and many came in family groups, exactly the audience we are attempting to build. I personally enjoyed, learned a tremendous amount and was humbled by sitting for hours in the gallery tracking and interviewing visitors as they walked through. I was struck by the very personal way that many visitors responded to the furniture, sharing stories with me about similar objects they remembered or grew up with. Humbling was the experience of seeing the occasional, uninterested visitor spend less than 30 seconds wandering through the gallery.

In conclusion, the Maryland Historical Society is thrilled with the important information obtained in this evaluation. As we continue to digest the

Institute for Learning Innovation's final report on *Baltimore Painted Furniture*, view visitors in the Museum and plan the MHS's new furniture and other galleries, I hope to continue expanding my insights on this valuable project. Look for the implementation of these results in our new building with its exhibitions of furniture, paintings and an overview of Maryland history due to open in the next three to five years.

I would like to recognize and thank the *Baltimore Painted Furniture* team members who worked so hard to make this exhibition and its revision a reality. Thank you Dale Jones, Nancy Davis, Dana Holland, Lynn Springer Roberts, Suzanne Rosenblum, Paul Rubenson, Janet Surrrett, Anne Verplank and Greg Weidman. Special thanks to Greg Weidman for so generously sharing her vast expertise on this subject and to Lynn Springer Roberts, project consultant, who tirelessly researched for this exhibition and continuously provided a national and international perspective to all of our work. Thanks also to Barbara Weeks and Heather Venters for all their multifaceted contributions. Lastly, thanks to Charles Davidson and Daniel Murphy of The Planning, Research and Design Group for their wonderfully inventive exhibition design which sets a high standard for the rest of the furniture galleries to follow.

ENDNOTES:

1. Falk, J.H. and Dierking, L.C. (2000). *Learning from Museums: Visitor Experiences and the Making of Meaning.* Walnut Creek, CA: AltaMira Press.

2. Percentages reported for various items do not equal 100 percent due to percentages of "no responses" for these items.

3. Serrell, B. (1996). *Exhibit Labels: An Interpretative Approach.* Walnut Creek, Ca.: AltaMira Press, 235.

4. Conversation with Marianna Adams, Senior Associate at the Institute for Learning Innovation, November 5, 1999.

5. Serrell, B. (1996), 234.

6. Serrell, B. (1996), 235

7. See Serrell, B. (1996) for an excellent description of how to write and produce exhibition labels.

8. Weidman, G. R. (1984). *Furniture in Maryland*, 1740-1940. Baltimore: Maryland Historical Society, and Weidman, G. R. et al. (1993). *Classical Maryland*, 1815-1845: *Fine and Decorative Arts from the Golden Age.* Baltimore: Maryland Historical Society.

SPNEA Takes a New Approach to an Old Building

Nancy Carlisle, Curator
Society for the Preservation of New England Antiquities

The Society for the Preservation of New England Antiquities is the nation's largest regional preservation organization, with 36 historic properties open to the public in five New England states. Over the course of its 90-year history, the Society has amassed a collection of some of the most intact historic interiors to survive anywhere. SPNEA's Sayward-Wheeler house in York, Maine, is arguably the most intact 18th century home in the country, with furnishings that were assembled and placed by Jonathan Sayward in the 1760s and 1770s. At Rundlet-May House in Portsmouth, New Hampshire, all of the systems installed in 1807 to ensure an up-to-date and well-run household—from a well room off the summer kitchen to a Rumford roaster and an elaborate venting system in the winter kitchen are still in place. Marrett House, situated at two crossroads in Standish, Maine, has the accumulated goods of several generations of a single family. While most of its rooms reflect layering over many years, the decorative scheme of the best parlor has remained unchanged since it was redecorated for a family wedding in 1847. Castle Tucker, also in Maine, is still furnished with the 14 wagonloads of furniture delivered from a ship on the river below in 1858. In fact, most of SPNEA's historic properties were donated to the Society complete with the families' furnishings and therefore contain the accumulated goods of multiple generations.

Given the innate historical integrity of the furnishings at most of SPNEA's properties, over the years the organization has become increasingly conservative in its interpretative approach. SPNEA's goal in most cases is for its stewardship to be as invisible as possible so that what visitors see reflects historical reality, unfiltered by curatorial intent.

There are exceptions, of course, and one of these is the subject of this paper. SPNEA's Spencer-Peirce-Little House, in Newbury, Massachusetts, is, in effect, a full-blown English manor house transplanted to the colonies; along with Bacon's Castle in Virginia, it is one of the most important surviving 17th century buildings in the country. It is a stone building, built around 1690 in an unusual cruciform plan, surrounded by rich agrarian lands. Newbury, on the coast north of Boston, was a successful agricultural and maritime community, and for 300 years this house has stood as testimony to that success.

The house and land came to SPNEA in 1986 after the death of the last owner. SPNEA's first task on receiving it was to undertake extensive architectural conservation. According to one architectural specialist who saw it at that time, it was in imminent danger of collapse, and was standing more by habit than anything else. Conservation was immediately undertaken and at the same time extensive documentation and interpretive planning began.

Like most of SPNEA's properties, this one came with the furnishings of the last family to occupy the house. The pieces in it had strong local histories, including inherited 18th century furniture made in the area, pieces bought at local auctions in the 19th century, and a few chairs found in the house when the family moved in. SPNEA's interpretive problem lay in the fact that the Littles did not move into the house until 1851, and their story—though interesting—reflected only half the property's history.

If SPNEA took its usual approach to the house—leaving the furnishings intact as the last owner left them—the absorbing story of some of the earlier occupants would be lost. The house's builder was Daniel Peirce, Jr. (1642-1704), a member of the Governor's Council of Massachusetts Bay and Newbury's wealthiest taxpayer, whose successful enterprises included farming, raising livestock, shipping fish to the West Indies, blacksmithing and maltmaking. Nathaniel Tracy (1751-1796), once one of Newbury's wealthiest residents, was forced to retire to the Spencer-Peirce-Little farm after his finances collapsed under post-Revolutionary embargoes and stringent trade laws. In addition to his wife and 11 children, his household included the freed slave Cupid Lee who had been part of Tracy's wife's dowry. The property's subsequent owner was Offin Boardman (1748-1811), a colorful patriot, renowned in the region for capturing

a British war ship during the Revolution. Boardman's diary survives and includes a graphic account of his escape from an English prison, where he was held for subsequent war activities, followed by his adventurous journey home via Paris. It also describes his family's lives as prosperous landowners at the Spencer-Peirce-Little farm at the turn of the 19th century. To show the house only as the Littles lived in it from the middle of the 19th century on would be to seriously shortchange the visitor.

There was also concern that if we left the interior furnished as it had been when the house came to us, we would somehow detract from the story of the building itself. The major significance of the architecture seemed to be a call for a different interpretive approach. After a long period of struggling with how best to present the house, the planning team suddenly realized that the interior architectural finishes inside lent themselves perfectly to a backwards walk through time. The first room visitors would enter—the dining room—was refurbished with colonial revival wallpapers and paint colors sometime in the middle of the 20th century. The next room—the kitchen—was upgraded around 1930, when electricity was installed but not changed afterwards. Next, the living room was refinished around 1860, and so on, all the way back to a chamber on the second floor with a circa 1690 chimney and plaster wall.

Once a backwards walk through time was determined as the organizing principle, we began to develop an interpretive plan. We were working with a set of challenges: how to provide visual clues to help people see that each room constituted a separate time period; how to tell them what SPNEA was doing to preserve the property (something visitor surveys told us visitors were interested in); how to honor SPNEA's preservation philosophy of being minimally invasive; and above all, how to convey a rich and complex narrative without losing the visitor. The plan we developed is being implemented incrementally over the course of several years and is now roughly half completed, with four of the six major rooms installed.

The first room we installed was the dining room, which was meant to appear as it did when the house came to SPNEA in 1986, and it is where we tell the dual story of the last generation to live in the house, and of SPNEA's stewardship efforts. In many ways, this was the easiest room to install, since, as the most recent, it required the least amount of conjecture. Because preparing the room furnishings was relatively simple, we were able to experiment with our interpretive approach.

All of SPNEA's tours are guided tours, but to reinforce the interpretive message the guide delivered in each room, we worked with designer Keith Ragone to develop a series of interpretive panels to help visitors identify what they were seeing; who lived in the house at the time; and how historians pull together the information that informs what the visitor sees. These panels are designed to be more visual than narrative, to complement the guide's discourse rather than compete with it. The first half of the panel shows who was living in the house at the time—owners, servants, tenant farmers, etc. The second half of the panel answers the question "How Do We Know?" In each room one type of historical record is discussed—historic photographs, oral histories, archaeology, documentary evidence, etc.

The more significant departure from traditional period room installations, aside from the use of interpretive panels, was the decision to install only a portion of each room as a vignette, leaving the area outside the vignette as it was when the house came to SPNEA. In part this was to accommodate SPNEA's preservation philosophy, which calls for the organization to preserve evidence of change over time. But vignettes are also a way to reinforce the artificial nature of what visitors are seeing. It is often the case that visual clues are stronger than verbal ones, so that visitors seeing a house in which each room is fully installed might think that they are seeing a house as someone had actually lived in it. We wanted to make it as clear as possible that what we were showing were various snippets of the house's history.

Because of the importance of the architectural story, there are architectural "viewports" throughout the house. Some show steel beams reinforcing the main framing members of the structure; others show wallpapers or wall treatments uncovered during the course of restoration. Guides also use additional visual aids, laminated historic photographs or conjectural drawings to help visitors understand what they are seeing.

SPNEA began installing a room a year at Spencer-Peirce-Little house beginning in 1996. Each year, as a new room was installed, we surveyed visitors to get their reactions and assessments of what they saw. This past year we decided to do a different type of survey to measure the effectiveness of the tour format at Spencer-Peirce-Little house. While previous surveys took place immediately

following a tour, this year we decided to test what people remembered some-time after their tour. We were looking for narrative rather than quantifiable responses, so the question we asked was purposefully open-ended. We mailed 500 post cards with the following text to visitors who had been to the property sometime in the past two years.

Tell us what you think!

If you have visited the Spencer-Peirce-Little Farm in Newbury, Mass. within the last year or two, we'd love to know what you remember about your trip. Spencer-Peirce-Little Farm is one of SPNEA's most recently opened properties, and we're interested to know how it's working. You can tell us anything, whether it's about the quality of light that day, or some-thing about the guide, or what you remember about the tour. Your answers will help us improve the work we do both at the farm and at other SPNEA properties. Thanks.

- *When did you visit the Spencer-Peirce-Little Farm?*
- *What do you remember about your visit?*

You can respond in three ways:

Visit the "What's New" section of SPNEA's web page www.SPNEA.org and fill in the questionnaire you find there. Drop a line to Nancy Carlisle, Curator and Manager of Collections, SPNEA 141 Cambridge St., Boston, MA 02114. Call Nancy Carlisle at (617) 227-3957, ext.237. If you prefer to call after hours, you can leave a message on Nancy's voice mail.

We knew that this was a completely unscientific survey and that therefore the results might not answer all of our questions. Even so, the responses were quite useful. Most of the responses came by phone or over the Web.

A number of respondents commented on the stunningly beautiful approach to the house. One wrote: "Just driving down the entry drive under the alleé of beautiful trees makes me feel as though I have stepped way back in time. It is so peaceful and lovely." Others commented on the quietness, or on the farming and the fields. A few other comments: "Horned larks and snow buntings"; "Mosquitoes"; "Airplanes overhead", "Mosquitoes the size of airplanes!" (Newbury is renowned for the ferociousness of its insect population.).

In terms of whether we are succeeding with our interpretation at Spencer-Peirce-Little house, not surprisingly, not a single respondent recalled a particular fact he or she had learned. But taken together the comments fall into a group of categories that suggest that overall, our approach is working. People commented about the walk through time, about the story of preservation, about the year-by-year installation and ongoing work being done by SPNEA, and about the unusual furnishing scheme.

What we hadn't anticipated, foolishly it now seems, since we take it so much for granted, was that virtually every respondent commented on the guide. All of the responses were highly favorable. "The guide was knowledgeable and enthusiastic. . . Totally delightful and informative. . . Articulate. . . poised . . . patient." The affirming thing for us is that we know the respondents were referring to several guides, and not just reacting to one extraordinarily talented one. This suggested we were successful in a way we hadn't even thought of measuring. SPNEA uses guides at all its properties largely to deliver information, but also to provide a measure of security without the need for intrusive barriers. We hadn't previously considered other ways that using guides might be successful for us.

This unexpected result led us to think about what exactly we were trying to measure to determine whether our interpretation was successful. In their seminal book *The Museum Experience*, authors John Falk and Lynn Dierking write that there is ample evidence that people do not learn in museums in a linear fashion, or in what they call "academic conceptual schemes."[1] Instead, what they suggest is that the learning that happens in museums is much more complex; it is "an interactive experience" that combines "social learning, concept learning, and aesthetic learning." This being so, clearly we should not be looking for factual learning in the responses to our survey.

In essence, what our respondents have told us is that what they most valued in their visit to Spencer-Peirce-Little farm was the tranquil beauty of the land, and the social interaction with an engaging and informative person. In effect, then, we were succeeding in ways we hadn't anticipated. Instead of traditional learning, it turns out that what people are gaining is a much broader and more memorable experience. This is about senses, and memory, and social interaction. Our challenge as curators and educators is to pay attention to the more holistic nature of the visitors' experiences, while still working to provide a meaningful educational dialogue. In doing so, we may reach even greater measures of success and open our portals to newly excited and challenged museumgoers.

ENDNOTES:

1. Falk, J. H. and Dierking, L. D. (1992). *The Museum Experience*. Washington, D.C.: Whalesback Books.

Making a New Home for the Decorative Arts in Newark: The Ballantine House

Ulysses Grant Dietz, Curator of Decorative Arts, The Newark Museum
Lucy Brotman, Director of Education, The Newark Museum
Timothy Wintemberg, Senior Exhibition Designer, The Newark Museum

When The Newark Museum unveiled its newly renovated complex in 1989, designed by renowned architect Michael Graves, the only new galleries allotted to the decorative arts collections were two small spaces fitted with built-in glass cases, and another small gallery designated the Contemporary Craft Gallery. This was not an oversight, and it turned out to be a golden opportunity for the decorative arts department and for the Museum as an institution. Attached to the Museum's "new" North Wing, built in 1926 as insurance company offices, was the 1885 Ballantine House, built for a Newark beer baron, and designated a National Historic Landmark in 1985. Since 1976, when five ground-floor period rooms had been restored as a Bicentennial project, the house had become one of the Museum's most popular attractions, and was the sole showcase for the Museum's large decorative arts holdings.[1] In the summer of 1989, when the executive offices in the renovated South Wing were completed, the Ballantine House's second floor was at last empty and ready to be turned over to the decorative arts department as its suite of permanent collection galleries.

That the period rooms would remain was a given, both from the curator's wishes and from popular demand. The Ballantine House is a rare survival, and a particularly rich example of Newark's halcyon days as one of the wealthiest industrial cities in the nation. As of 1989, the plans tacitly agreed to by the curator and the administration for the house were to restore three front rooms on the second floor—because the public had always wanted to see bedrooms—and to use the rest of the upstairs rooms as furniture galleries, divided generally by chronological period. The ground-floor lecture room, which had been made in the 1920s by combining the original kitchen and billiard room, would be redivided into two spaces: a restored billiard room, and a silver gallery, fitted with cases like those in the adjacent new Michael Graves galleries (which were designated for ceramics and glass). This plan seemed to be the most logical way to allot space to various key aspects of the decorative arts holdings.

The curator, who had studied the decorative arts collections while at Yale University, and then gotten his Early American Material Culture degree from the Winterthur Program at the University of Delaware, had a very clear, traditional vision of how objects should be displayed and how labels should be written. He also had virtually no experience of working in close collaboration with either a designer or an educator before an exhibition. The traditional mode of operation was for a curator to select objects, write labels, then submit them first to the exhibitions department to figure out how to install them, and then to the education department to determine the best way to build a program around them.

Had Newark been a richer museum, or had the 1976 restoration of the Ballantine House been more than cosmetic, things might well have proceeded as outlined above. However, the project faced a major roadblock in 1989—the house itself. Relying on its 1926 commercial boilers and window air-conditioning units, the house could not come close to sustaining a stable climate. Additionally, the house was damp in both attic and cellar, and leaked both soot and air copiously through loose, century-old windows. Since the main collections focused in these spaces were to be furniture and silver, it was clear that climate control was essential. In fact, it was obvious that the house needed to be brought up to the same standards as the new "state of the art" museum complex to which it was attached.

From the initial concept of repainting the galleries and adding a few air conditioners, the Ballantine House project quickly grew into something that was going to cost upwards of $4 million. This daunting prospect, coming on the heels of a $23 million capital project, again turned out to be a lucky break. For the climate control part of the project, the Museum successfully applied to the National Endowment for the Humanities' Preservation of Collections program, and was lucky enough to get a substantial matching grant. For the historical preservation of the house itself, the New Jersey Historic Trust provided a generous source of funding—with all the restrictions implied in working on an historic structure. The keystone of this entire project was, however, the initial approach made by the Lila Wallace Readers' Digest Fund. The Fund was seeking to implement a new Collections Accessibility Initiative, aimed at urban museums across the country, to try to assist them in getting under-used collections out of storage and presenting them to under-served audiences. The Newark Museum was invited to be among the first applicants for this initiative, competing for grants of up to $1.5 million.

So far so good. The catch was that we needed to come up with a new way to present our collections, and a new way to involve our curatorial, education and design staff throughout the process. Finally, we had to be able to demonstrate how this new exhibition program and new method of arriving there was not only sensitive to the needs of the Museum's wider community, but also how it was going to transform the institution itself. This is gross oversimplification, but it gives a clear sense of how difficult this process was going to be.

The first thing we did was scrap all of the curator's old notions. Gone were the old-fashioned silver gallery[2] and the furniture galleries. The new period rooms would remain, but we needed to figure out how to interpret them and the whole Ballantine House more effectively. Additionally, we needed to figure out how the broad range of objects in the decorative arts collections (ranging from 16th-century Italy to the present day) could possibly connect coherently with a late Victorian beer baron's city mansion. We needed a team. Two teams, actually. The home team was made up of the curator; the Director of Education, Susan A. Newberry; the Assistant Director of Education, Lucy Brotman; and an Exhibition Designer, Tim Wintemberg. Then we created what we came to call the away team. For thematic development, we chose Gretchen Sullivan Sorin, now the Director of the Cooperstown Graduate Program in Museum Studies. Gretchen not only has a long history dealing with museums seeking to address minority issues in their exhibitions, but is a Newark native, and thus knew the city. For a curatorial perspective that would support but depart from the curator's own viewpoint, we chose Michael J. Ettema, then an Associate Curator of Domestic Life at Henry Ford Museum & Greenfield Village. Finally, for design development as well as thematic assistance, we found James Sims, then at the International Center of the Smithsonian Institution, now an independent design consultant.

The second thing we did was to arrange a focus group study, using the services of ArtsMarket, out of Marion, Massachusetts. The Ballantine House had just been closed when the focus group took place, but nothing had yet been removed from the rooms. Two days of live interviews, covering four carefully selected groups from among the Museum's diverse audience constituencies, were videotaped and monitored from another room by the home team.

Hovering over this focus group study was a recent incident that was vivid in all of the home team's minds: a school teacher from a nearby inner-city community (not, incidentally, Newark itself) had complained eloquently that she saw no reason to bring her mostly poor, mostly minority students into a grand house that was built for long-dead, rich white people. She could not understand how this could possibly be relevant to the lives of her young pupils. Although the home team—and specifically the educators—did not agree with her opinion, we all understood the implicit challenge in this incident. How *do* you make a rich family's mansion relevant to *anyone* in modern-day America, much less people for whom all the house's baroque extravagance might seem a slap in the face? These words echoed in our minds as we watched the focus groups on closed-circuit television, and later reviewed the eight hours of videotape. ArtsMarket produced a distillation of the study, which became our prime jumping-off point in determining what our project would be for the Lila Wallace Readers' Digest Fund proposal.

The good news is that all of the focus groups loved the Ballantine House. They loved the sense of time travel that it gave—of stepping back into Victorian Newark. They loved the visual richness (even if they didn't want to live that way) and the amazing quality of the craftsmanship (*"This was all made in Newark?"*). What they didn't like were the Plexiglas label holders, weighted down with long citations from Victorian etiquette books and decorating guides. They wanted to know about the *family*. They wanted to know what the house *meant* to them, and to the people around them. They wanted to know how the rooms were used by the family. They didn't like the use of the little Music Room as a changing decorative arts gallery (the curator winced over this) because it broke the flow of the time-travel experience. They loved the idea of more period rooms, and being able to climb the grand ornate staircase, past the huge stained glass window on the landing.

The bad news was that no one in any of the four focus groups could properly define what the term decorative arts meant. Even for knowledgeable collectors and our consultants, it was nearly impossible to create a succinct definition for this pervasive term. Also, the general feeling was that people wanted the entire house restored, and did not particularly want thematic galleries devoted to the range of the decorative arts holdings. The first point we paid attention to; the second, we advisedly chose to ignore, although we did sacrifice the Music Room gallery to keep the ground floor experience whole. We felt that the benefits to be derived from the display of a broad chronological and aesthetic range of the collections were far greater than yet more period bedrooms. Getting collections out of storage was, after all, the crux of the grant proposal.

The first step was convincing the Lila Wallace Fund people that this was a worthy project. It was perhaps the most difficult grant application ever experienced by anyone on the home team. Amazingly, except for details and the final choices made in terms of technological exhibitry, the application as submitted remained remarkably close to the final exhibition. One important detail that the team arrived at early on was the title, *House & Home*. The driving notion was that the reason this museum owned all of these objects, ranging from 16th-century Urbino majolica to 1950s Pyrex cookware, was that each and every one of them had *come from someone's home*. Someone, somewhere, for some reason, had chosen every one of these 20,000 objects for use in their home. It was in the 19th century, we realized, that the separation of the terms "house" and "home" began to take on the heavily loaded connotations that they continue to hold today. It was, moreover, in the 19th century that industrialization really began to transform the American majority population known generically as the "middle class" into a vast marketplace of consumers. We posited, somewhat nervously, that even though the Ballantine House was built for a millionaire family, it could still be interpreted as representative of American middle-class values in the late 19th century. The Ballantines, like any other middle-class American family, expressed their cultural values in their home, and chose objects to fill their rooms that physically and visually demonstrated who they were and what they believed in. They just had a much bigger budget. Their house, in essence, was a "dream house"—the ideal home.

Well, the Lila Wallace Fund liked the idea and we were awarded $1.5 million, half of which could go towards things like climate control and sprinklers, and half of which had to be devoted to implementing the ambitious reinterpretive scheme we had imagined. It was the largest single grant the Museum had ever received for any project. From this moment forward, Mary Sue Price, the Museum's director, became the combined teams' greatest cheerleader and toughest critic. It was her role to bring all of the Museum's trustees and funders on board for the new interpretive program, and also rein in the home and away teams when we began to stray too far outside the lines of our Museum's mission.

The complex process of creating a new home for the decorative arts collection was grueling, although there were many moments of hilarity and an enormous amount of intellectual exhilaration. The away team turned out to be just the right mixture of sympathy and divisiveness. They challenged existing curatorial notions of what objects mean and how people perceive them, and they forced the curator to accept as equal partners his educator and designer teammates. The away team produced vast quantities of provocative ideas for how to display objects, how to group objects and how to interpret objects. In the final phase of the project, the home team worked alone, in consultation with various community members, to figure out what we could fit into the distinctly restricted space afforded by even so large a house as the Ballantine House. In retrospect, we ultimately had to discard many of the ideas we had thought up with the consultants, but the luxury of being able to spend so much time coming up with a new way to interpret an old collection was extraordinary, and something we shall likely not experience again.

An imperative of the Lila Wallace Fund stipulated that the institution change as the project was achieved. And there is no question that this project did change the way home team members worked within the institution and with their colleagues. While the curator was the chief author and selected the objects to be included, the educators and designer became copy editors and content editors, and truly shaped the final product to suit what we all felt to be the needs of our diverse audiences. Thus, the Lila Wallace Fund imperative that the institution change as part of the project was achieved.

The *House & Home* project was essentially divided into three sections: the Orientation Gallery (in the space built as the kitchen and larders in 1885); the Period Rooms; and the Thematic Galleries. The Orientation Gallery would introduce all of the big ideas related to the ideal home that would be repeated in different ways throughout the rest of the exhibit. The Period Rooms would provide a case study of one family's fulfillment of the ideal home fantasy at one historic moment (1891). The Thematic Galleries would reexamine key themes related to the ideal home, using objects from all time periods to demonstrate the main points.

One of the first things the home and away teams did was to wrestle with the term "decorative arts." After many attempts to try to "demystify" the term, we realized that we needed simply to eliminate the term altogether. Decorative arts, for the purpose of the public, simply became home furnishings. The second thing we did was to realize that we wanted to offer many different ways to approach the objects and the period rooms, and to vary "information delivery" from gallery to gallery as well. We knew that the audiences we were trying to reach would all come to the Museum with different expectations and different interests. It sounds a little like trying to be all things to all people, but nonetheless that was our goal, and by some miracle it seems to have mostly worked. We did eventually create in our minds a model target audience: minority people, both urban and suburban, in their 30s and 40s, bringing children between the ages of 8 and 13 with them to the Museum. This was not at all the only audience we expected to visit the house, but it was the audience we wanted to make sure received a happy, satisfying and educational experience.

Throughout the *House & Home* installation we created printed text in varying sizes of type. Extremely large "banner" headlines in every gallery provide, in relatively few words, the entire gist of the exhibition. If one visitor spent ten minutes walking through the galleries and read only these large words, he would get the idea. Then we had text panels and fixed labels of a smaller scale, which built a more complicated picture of what home means, and how objects fulfilled people's notions of the ideal home. Finally, for the audience we fondly referred to as "object weenies," we created flip books and notebooks with comparative images and basic information on every one of the some 1,500 objects included in the galleries and period rooms. We avoided throughout terms like "rare" and "important," even though this caused the curator some mental distress. We had to admit that such terminology is, first of all, the typical way in which museums try to tell their visitors that they *must* like and admire something. Our goal was to de-emphasize rarity and focus more on the meaning of the object in the home. We did not want to seem to tell our visitors that they had to like something just because it was on view in our Museum. All we wanted to do was to try to help them understand *why* it was in our collection. Secondly, we knew from visitor studies that most museum audiences really don't care if something is rare or important (unless it happens to be a famous object in some specific way, such as the Lincoln Chair at Henry Ford Museum). Only curators, collectors and antiques dealers really care about this sort of subtle status. The curator finally accepted that his peers—the people for whom, like it or not, art museum curators traditionally write their labels—would figure out rarity and importance on their own. The general public really just wanted to know *why*.

We also realized, especially with the help of our away team, that we needed to get away from the omnipresent "museum voice," and to arrive at some way to create a range of voices that would present a more varied reality. Not only voices of the curator, but of the object's maker, owner, inheritor and even caretaker. We wanted to demonstrate the fact that the *value* of an object is in its meaning, and that this value can vary widely from person to person. We hoped to allow the visitor to engage with an object by inviting him to think about his own feelings about that object—rather than just accept, as given, the Museum's opinion.

Sometimes creating these "voices" was a literal process—making up quotations for a specific object that would show the various viewpoints of different people at the time of its creation, or over the entire span of its lifetime until it entered the Museum. In other cases, the voice was nothing more than the inclusion of objects that came from minority families. This was a simple, but deeply significant institutional change affecting collecting policy. Knowing about the ethnic background of an object's history of ownership—Irish, Jewish, African-American, Italian-American, etc.—suddenly became a key facet in understanding the object's significance. People's ability to find glimpses of themselves in these galleries was going to be a key way to open them up to understanding the bigger thematic issues.

The Orientation Gallery was the most difficult single space for which to write the script. Ultimately it took many revisions to hone in on the crucial words that would lead visitors into the Ballantine House rooms and upstairs into the Thematic Galleries: House, Ideal Home, Work, Family, Shopping. Graphic images from various sources were used more heavily in this space than anywhere else in the exhibit (or anywhere in the Museum). A blow-up of an 1830s painting of a Newark chairmaker's house, workshop and sales room—all side by side—evoked the pre-industrial reality of the American home. In contrast, a late 1850s lithograph by Currier & Ives called "Home Sweet Home," set against a huge mural of a furniture factory, evoked a romantic suburban vision and the separation of home from the workplace that embodies the ideal home as it still exists today. Beneath these two color photo blow-ups are large displays of objects, each arranged as if in a store window, and each representing the kinds of objects that pre-industrial and industrial middle-class Americans would have expected (or simply desired) to own. At one end of the gallery is a deep niche, on which two pieces of Newark-made furniture of the 1850s and 1860s sit in front of a mural of a Grand Rapids furniture showroom from the 1870s. Here shopping (i.e., choosing) is introduced, along with both the idea of accessibility of ready-made furnishings for a wide class of Americans and the ongoing importance of this kind of shopping in contemporary American culture.

Finally, at the entrance to the Ballantine House proper (the visitor does not know he is in the kitchen until he enters the second gallery space), large images of Newark in the 1890s (home as part of community and neighborhood as context for home) begin to set the stage for the case study of the Ballantine House as one family's dream house in one place in one time. The cinematic image we were trying to create was a distant bird's-eye view of the city of Newark, with the camera sweeping down and in, narrowing the focus from city to neighborhood to street to home, to household, not unlike the introductory images from a television series.

Because the period rooms required their own sort of orientation, and their own kind of multi-level interpretive materials, we started with all sorts of visual material in the Orientation Gallery. At one level we wanted to express the function of the back door, through which you enter the house, as a sort of "social filter" that was used by certain people for certain reasons—as differentiated from the front door. We also wanted to take this opportunity to make it clear that most Americans could not afford the ideal home in its entirety, and even that some Americans didn't (or couldn't) buy the kind of home furnishings that the visitor would see in the galleries. We differentiated between the "ideal" and the reality of the day. We also included a facsimile of a rare 1911 census map of Newark, delineating in great detail all of the diverse ethnic and racial groups that made up the city.

We posited that our visitors might have different expectations in entering the house. One group was looking for the fantasy of traveling back in time to peek at life in the past. A second group was looking for a practical story of what each room was for. The third (and probably smallest) group was there to see old objects rather than the old house. The Period Rooms each had three "information delivery systems" attached to the label rails to address these three imagined visitor groups. The storybooks are placed on the left side, each fabricated in the actual 3D form of a large book with a red cover. At the center of each room is a more traditional "curator's voice" panel with a brief heading related to the function of the room, along with four color images which are details of key objects that explain the purpose of the room. This, in theory, gives the average visitor just enough curatorial input to think more about the individual objects within each rich assemblage of things. Finally, on the right are notebooks, which are loose-leaf, and include laminated plastic pages showing period illustrations of similar rooms, as well as a complete inventory of every object in the room, with basic identifying information. Most people don't bother with this book, but it is there for those who want the information.

The label rails themselves were carefully designed with ADA requirements in mind. They are low enough for a seven-year-old child to see over easily, but comfortable for a person in a wheelchair. All of the type is large and easy to read from ten feet away. The viewing bays themselves were enlarged to allow visitors to really enter the rooms rather than just stand huddled in the doorway. This required that we add an elaborate electronic security system that would counter-balance the easier physical access to the rooms.

But the crucial element in the Period Rooms was the introduction of the storybook panels. Thinking madly of some way to lure school-aged children into caring about those dark, fussy, Victorian rooms, the team hit upon the idea of the comic strip. This was a means to tell a story without introducing either costumed interpreters or static mannequins. Although there was some mildly hysterical talk about holographic projections, we soon saw that low-tech would be best. Then, as the script evolved, and we realized that there wasn't really any action in any of the rooms, we reduced it to larger single illustrations, which took on the form and feel of a large-scale Victorian illustration as if from a novel. We intentionally sought out an artist (Dan Krovatin, from Trenton) who could evoke the style of celebrated late Victorian illustrator Charles Dana Gibson.

One note must be made here. The Newark Museum is an art museum, not a history museum. Thus our mission in interpreting our collections in the context of an historic house was not to create a historical reality, but to create a theatrical setting which was historically authentic and plausible. Many of our objects come without histories—they were acquired for reasons of style or craftsmanship. Thus, while we knew we were doing something radical in terms of art museums, we also understood that we were doing something that a history museum might not feel comfortable with either. In the end, it was the public's experience that was our greatest concern.

The storybooks are dialogues between two characters who are shown together in each of the rooms. The entire "cast" is introduced in the Orientation Gallery, with an explanation that some are real and some are fictitious. They are shown, in a colored illustration of the same Gibsonesque style, all lined up as if for a publicity photograph. Thus, the stage is set for a series of nine mini-dramas. The visitor (if he or she reads the introductory material, which is entirely optional) is assigned the role of someone delivering something to the butler, and ushered into the house through the back door by Bridget, the chambermaid (in a storybook set in the backyard). Thus, the visitor is encouraged to explore the rooms to find out what's going on. If he remembers that he was supposedly looking for the butler by the time he finds him, so much the better. But the story need not be linear, nor must the rooms be seen in any order.

Each dialogue is brief, taking less than a minute to read, and encourages visitors to interact with each other in reading it. In these short dramatic moments, fictional or historical characters associated with the house discuss whatever they are doing at that moment. In this way they manage to convey to the reader not only the meaning of the particular room in which they are situated, but also some broader and more complex social reality tied to the notion of home in general and the Ballantine House in particular. Far more effectively than an omniscient curator's declaration, these concise dialogues illuminate interpersonal relationships as well as prevailing cultural attitudes. For example, in the Billiard Room we find 16-year-old Alice Ballantine and a friend discussing a party they plan to have in that room. Not only do they need to deal with how to disguise the ugly "maleness" of the room (the spittoon, the animal heads), but their short chat brings up issues of gender expectations for upper-class girls, and changing gender roles in the late Victorian home.

In each Period Room the two characters were chosen to be both historically plausible and also to be somewhat surprising. In the parlor, which was Mrs. Ballantine's domain, the visitor encounters a conversation between two female servants: one a teenage Irish kitchen maid for whom the parlor is alien territory, the other a German parlor maid who knows every object intimately, *but not as the owner.* In the reception room we've placed an African-American couple who are waiting to speak to Mrs. Ballantine about a charitable donation. Although the situation is fictitious, the couple, Mr. and Mrs. James Baxter, are real. Mr. Baxter was the principal of the Negro School in Newark, his wife was a teacher, and both were pillars of St. Philip's Episcopal Church, the Negro parish in Newark.[4] As they wait for the lady of the house, they manage to cover everything from their own comfortable home just a few blocks away, to the marginal status of middle-class black people in America. The purpose here was multiple. The first was to explain what a reception room was for, by making it the scene of a social ritual that was central to Victorian etiquette—a formal call to solicit a donation to church missionary work. The second was to demonstrate that it was not only wealthy people who ascribed to the value system that valued polite behavior and nice homes. Thirdly, it was to underscore the historical reality of a middle-class black community in Newark and, by extrapolation, in America. Few visitors to the Ballantine House, black or white, expect to find an African-American couple as part of the exhibition, and the surprise of this discovery makes the experience more memorable. However, we were careful to determine that the presence of this couple, even if it never actually took place, was plausible. We learned from social historians, for example, that even a well-dressed, educated black man would probably not have been allowed into the Ballantine House without a female escort. We also knew that Mrs. Ballantine would have known who Mr. Baxter was and, however she might have felt, would have treated him with courtesy and respect.

The library's storybook focuses on two boys playing at Cowboys and Indians. In their brief conversation they manage to explain both the family's cultural and educational values, as well as the misinformation that can be taught to children (in this case regarding American Indians). They also, quite simply, are behaving like children (they're building a fort with a tablecloth and some well-placed objects). In the dining room we at last find the butler, Mr. McAllister, who is setting the table for dinner with the waitress, Margaret. They are talking about this evening's guests, who include Mr. and Mrs. Louis Plaut, who own Newark's largest department store. Here the issue is also double-barreled—the complex game of dinner-table etiquette in the high Victorian era as well as the interaction between wealthy Jewish people and their non-Jewish peers in a city like Newark.

All of the storybooks were edited extensively by the other members of the home team, usually during meetings in the curator's office with lots of good-natured yelling. Additionally, the historical and linguistic plausibility were vetted through historians and literature professors, to make sure that the language had a ring of truth, and that its authenticity would make it memorable to visitors. Descendants of the Baxters were asked to approve both their story-book and their picture (in fact we had to change the woman in the story from Baxter's teenage daughter to his wife, Pauline, because the daughter would have been too young in 1891). The Museum's volunteer docents also were asked to read the storybooks, in order to get their perspective. At this point in the process, newly appointed Deputy Director for Programs and Collections Ward Mintz served as a sort of diplomatic envoy between the home team and the various constituent groups who were being asked to comment on the exhibition script. His skill at working out compromises and smoothing ruffled feathers was enormously helpful for a project team that had gotten rather frayed at the edges.

The Music Room, which had been restored in 1976 but furnished as a gallery with four illuminated cases, was transformed into a hands-on interactive gallery called "Make yourself at home." Its purpose was to drive home the point that, forbidding as it might be, a house like the Ballantine House was meant to be *comfortable* and was intended for a family. It was not a palace, it was a home. Knowing that the room was really a small sitting room for the family (for when they were shut out of the library while Mr. Ballantine worked at his desk), the room was furnished with non-collection pieces, including a desk, a large mirror, a china cupboard and a reproduction Morris chair and footstool copied from actual pieces in the adjacent library. Thus, people can pull reproduction toys and retail catalogues off the shelves in the china cupboard, settle back in the easy chair, rifle through the photocopied papers on the desk, and look at color-copied magazines and other period publications on a side table. People can also try on various pieces of "period" clothing, and look at themselves in a big Victorian cheval glass. Text panels on the walls posed questions about the room. The Education Department is charged with monitoring and replacing lost pieces of hands-on material. While the photocopied documents do disappear with some regularity, the public treatment of the room is remarkably gentle.[5]

The second floor is reached by means of the staircase. Wide and easy to climb, it offers a marvelous sense of procession, either up or down. We were very fortunate that, because the Museum is attached to the house physically, all of the difficult ADA requirements—like bathrooms and wheelchair access to each floor by elevator—could be handled outside the walls of the historic structure. Luckily, the 1885 house has very wide doors, so that was never a problem in terms of wheelchair access. But once you ascend the stairs, the program begins to change.

There are storybooks on the second floor. The wide staircase landing, beneath the stained glass window that rises 13 feet above a leather-covered banquette, is where the visitor first encounters John and Jeannette Ballantine. They are seen in a pair of large three-quarter-length portraits done by a French academic

painter in 1890, and hanging in their original location at either side of the landing. These paintings, however, are interpreted through the eyes of Bridget, the Irish chamber maid, who marvels at their $8,000 combined cost, and realizes that if she's ever going to own a home of her own, she'll have to leave the Ballantines. In fact, all of the storybooks on the second floor—the Master Bedroom, Mrs. Ballantine's Boudoir, and Alice Ballantine's Bedroom—are voiced as monologues, brief soliloquies about some aspect of life in 1891. So, to round off the storybook theme, we hear the private thoughts of a man, a woman, a girl, and a servant, each expressing something about what this house means to them.

The Thematic Galleries are housed in either semi-restored rooms or in renovated spaces. In each case we included wall texts, usually small, on the entrance door or near the entrance to the room, explaining what function these rooms originally served in 1885. This at least allows those who want nothing but the historic house to complete their tour. But the four galleries are simply extrapolations on ideas already encountered by the visitors. They each ask a question—to which there is no right or wrong answer, only a personal response.

- Are we doing the "right" thing?
- Do things make us a family?
- Are we comfortable yet?
- How do we choose things for our home?

Within each gallery, a range of objects, roughly chronological, explores different aspects of the broad theme. The dual agenda of the object choices here was to let the curator put out his favorite and/or most important objects and to incorporate objects with compelling stories that related to the gallery themes. In the "Right Thing" gallery, the objects speak to issues of etiquette (behavioral rules), gender roles, fashion and education. In the "Family" gallery, all of the objects in some way express family connections, whether it be children, marriage, death, or simply the concept of the "heirloom." In the "Comfort" gallery, which was originally the Guest Room, issues of comfort—storage, lighting, heating and seating—are illustrated with collection objects. Here the underlying theme is that most of what modern Americans of all economic levels take for granted in their homes—comfort, warmth, light, plumbing—were once considered luxuries, and that it was the rise of the concept of home in the 19th century that made these luxuries into necessities.

Several objects in different parts of these galleries have been set aside with complex "voice" labels, in which different perspectives on the piece are given. For example, an elaborate rococo revival étagère from the 1850s is given two sets of multiple voices. In one, a range of people in the year it was made express their feelings—from the seller to the buyer's husband, to their daughter and their

parlor maid, to the German-born woodcarver who made the piece but could never afford to own it. In the second, the same piece is seen through the eyes of different people over time—from the maker, to the auctioneer in the 1930s who shudders at its Victorian bad taste, to the 1980s curator who praises it just the way its maker did back in the 1850s. There are many ways to see an object, and no one way is the *only* way. Of course, the curator was simply pleased to have one of his most important objects out on view.

The final theme gallery serves a double purpose. "How do we choose things for our home?" is immediately above the Orientation Gallery, in the former servants' wing of the house. It is also the access point to the house from the second floor art galleries, and thus, for good or for ill, becomes the space through which many people enter the house. Thus this gallery had to serve as a secondary orientation, and thus, its theme about choice. Here objects are arranged on platforms and in cases (furniture of varying forms and tea sets), covering a time range from Colonial to Contemporary. Placed on the walls and in the cases are the kinds of timeless questions that people who are furnishing a home ask. What do I need? What can I afford? What style do I like? And so forth. Recently, because the curator and educators felt that people weren't connecting, the furniture platforms were reinstalled, and new label stands with flip-labels were added. These labels pose questions about pieces in the gallery, which require the visitor to guess which piece fits which question. When the label is flipped up, the visitor finds the answers with a color image of the piece and a brief historical nugget about the history of the object.[6] Making people flip over the labels seems to be one of the surest ways to make them read the labels. These new labels were modeled on those in the "Right Thing" gallery, which were a hit from the day the installation opened. The laminated labels (which can be produced in-house) need routine replacement because they get so much use.

Also in this gallery are two computer stations, featuring "Make Room," an interactive computer game designed and produced by James Sims and his post-Smithsonian business, Threshold Studios. Using images of objects from the Museum's collection—many but not all of which are in the galleries—an imaginary house is presented. There are seven galleries to explore, in which objects are arranged by style—a chair, a table, a case piece, and a textile or pattern. A huge attic atop the house is full of random selections of these objects, which can be chosen and taken to an empty room, and arranged as the player wishes. Simply seen, this was a way to get adolescent boys to play house without getting squeamish. It allows the visitor, using museum objects, to consider what they like and don't like, and what might or might not go together in a room. There is no winning or losing here, and the result is always the right one. Although the technology on this game is a little bit slow by today's standards, the premise—a way to offer more and different information about household furnishings and what they mean to people—is both sound and successful.

The final feature of the *House & Home* experience is a nine-minute video called "Home is in the Heart," set in a small curtained-off space just off the top of the staircase. Here the goal was purely emotional, although there is didactic content as well. The basic idea—using a motherly African-American narrator combined with a rich melange of contemporary, live interviews and vivid period images—was to draw emotional connections between the Victorian home and the modern home. The producers, Newark MediaWorks, used local New Jersey people of wide-ranging diversity to express their ideas about house and home. The result is simple, satisfying and reinforces the idea that the great, grand, fancy Ballantine House might not be such an alien thing after all. While, for many practical reasons, we did not have bilingual labels elsewhere in the installation, the film is offered in English and Spanish and is close-captioned.

A subsequent addition to the house is a special holiday interpretive scheme called *Christmas in the Ballantine House: Feasting with Family and Friends*. In this we slightly rearrange the Parlor and the Dining Room to represent a neighborhood open house tea on Christmas Eve and Christmas Dinner with the family. New storybook dialogues were written (using the same characters and images), and new interpretive "dive sheets" (laminated panels that can be dropped into special holders on the label rails) created to discuss the different context. This seasonal installation draws an additional and traditional holiday audience, while reiterating in yet another way the essential themes of *House & Home*.

The Ballantine House *House & Home* project is not complete. In the five years since it opened, it has been tinkered with, and various proposals for modifying bits of it have been drafted. It will continue to evolve. Also, unfortunately, we have never done formal audience evaluation on *House & Home*, because the Lila Wallace Readers' Digest Fund has subsequently focused on the Museum as an overall test case for its programs. Thus most of our evaluation of the installation is internal and anecdotal. From that perspective, the installation has accomplished everything we hoped it would. Rich and not-so-rich, urban, suburban, and rural, families, couples and singles—people of all kinds—seem to enjoy going through the various rooms and galleries, and all seem to take away something personal. There have been virtually no complaints about any of the interpretive strategies since the house opened. Everyone can find something they like somewhere in the galleries, something that validates them and echoes their own feelings.

But one thing remains clear—it was a radical departure for this collection and this Museum staff when it first began, and it has forever changed the way we present ourselves to our public and our funders.

ENDNOTES:

1. These holdings include some 20,000 objects: furniture, metalwork, ceramics, glass, costumes and textiles, dolls and toys.

2. We did eventually receive some NEH funding for the cases originally conceived of for this gallery, but were allowed to use that money for the large case that was ultimately designed for the Orientation Gallery.

3. It will be interesting to see how telecommuting eventually alters this reality. However, people who work at home for a larger company "out there" are still separating work from home, and we don't think this deeply ingrained mental and cultural construct is going to fade away fast.

4. Not only is Baxter a key figure in local history curricula in Newark City Schools, but there is a chapel dedicated to St. Philip's in the Episcopal cathedral.

5. This paper does not deal with the adult and school group educational programs. Our volunteer docents were trained in three different adult tours while the staff educators were trained in three different school tours for different age groups. The curator maintains an informal internal newsletter updating docents and educators about changes in the house and new interpretive concepts.

6. New computer capabilities and a digital camera have made inserting such color images inexpensive and easy to do.

The Hillwood Museum & Gardens Visitor Studies: 1995–1997

Randi Korn, President, Randi Korn & Associates, Inc.

Preface:

The Hillwood Museum & Gardens, Washington, D.C., is "one of America's premier estate museums, featuring the largest assemblage of imperial Russian fine and decorative arts outside Russia, and an extensive collection of 18th-century French works of art."[1] The estate's founder was Marjorie Merriweather Post, heir of the Post cereal empire. In 1995 Hillwood staff members started investigating their audience, in part because they were awarded an NEH self-study grant, but also because their strategic plan outlined an ambitious agenda to restore the House (where the collections are displayed) and to construct a new visitor center. The Museum would close for about two years, and during that time staff would reinvent the Museum and the visitor experience. To provide visitors with a new experience, they had to understand visitors' current experiences. Because the institution had never examined its audience, the first step was to conduct basic audience research. Two other visitor studies followed— observations of visitors taking a guided tour[2] of the house and interviews with visitors after they completed their tour; and focus groups with tour takers several months after their experience.

This paper presents a summary of all three studies along with recommendations made by the consultant, Randi Korn & Associates, Inc. The presentation style of the summaries, discussions and recommendations changed over time, as the type of study that was conducted, in part, dictated the presentation style of each report. These studies have provided Hillwood with concrete information about their visitors, and staff has used this information to create new and exciting interpretive programs.

The Hillwood Museum: Audience Profile

The following are findings from a mail-back visitor survey conducted at the Hillwood Museum. The questionnaire was designed to provide staff members with a demographic profile of visitors, information about what visitors do at Hillwood, and an assessment of visitors' experiences. Specifically, the goals of the Hillwood visitor survey were to determine:

- visitors' demographic characteristics, including group composition;

- visitors' behaviors, including how visitors first hear about Hillwood, why they visit Hillwood, and what they do once they are there;
- visitors' experiences;
- visitors' suggestions for improving their visit;
- visitors' self-rating of their knowledge of certain subjects.

A total of 968 visitors returned completed questionnaires.

Demographics:

- More women (81.2 percent) than men (18.8 percent) visit the Hillwood Museum.
- The mean age of visitors is 52 years. Almost three-quarters of visitors are 45 years of age and older.
- Three-quarters of visitors are college educated (76 percent). More than one-third have a graduate degree (36 percent), but more Saturday visitors have a graduate degree than weekday visitors.
- Nearly all visitors to Hillwood are white (95 percent).
- Nearly all visitors reside in the United States (96 percent). More than half reside in the District of Columbia, Maryland and Virginia (59 percent).
- The annual family income of more than one-third of visitors is $100,000 or more. About one-quarter of visitors have an annual family income of $50,000 – $74,999 (25 percent).

Visiting Behaviors:

- Nearly three-quarters of visitors hear about Hillwood from a "friend/relative" (74 percent).
- Nearly three-quarters travel to Hillwood by car (73 percent).
- Nearly three-quarters come in groups of 2-4 visitors (71 percent). Most visitors visit Hillwood with one or more companions (96 percent).
- Nearly three-quarters of visitors are first-time visitors (75 percent). More repeat visitors live in the District of Columbia, Maryland and Virginia than live in other parts of the United States.
- The majority of visitors visit Hillwood "to see the Main House" (78 percent) and "to see the Russian collection" (58 percent). "To see the Russian collection," however, varies according to frequency of visit.
- Nearly all visitors "tour the Main House" (91 percent) and "view the orientation movie" (89 percent). However, more older visitors tour the Main House than do younger visitors, and more first-time visitors tour the Main House than do repeat visitors. Visits to the Main House also vary according to month of visit and age.

- More visitors visit the gardens/greenhouse on Saturdays than on weekdays, and more younger visitors visit the gardens/greenhouse than do older visitors. Visits to the gardens/greenhouse also vary according to month of visit and day of visit.

- Nearly three-quarters of visitors make their own tour reservations (73 percent). More than half of those visitors rate getting a space on the tour a 5 on the difficult (1)/easy (5) scale (60 percent).

- Visitors report that they would most likely visit Hillwood on weekend days (63 percent) and weekdays (60 percent). However, these findings vary according to month of visit, day of visit and age. For example, older visitors would be more likely to visit on weekdays, and younger visitors would be more likely to visit on weekday evenings, weekend days and weekend evenings.

Visitors' Experience Ratings:

- The majority of visitors' experiences on the tour are "interesting," "informative," "comfortable" and "manageable," although the ratings for "comfortable" and "manageable" are not as high as they are for "interesting" and "informative." Thus, visitors find the tour more "interesting" and "informative" than "comfortable" and "manageable." However, visitors' experiences on the tour vary according to day of visit, age and education level.

- More than half the visitors think the length of the tour is just right, as 56 percent of visitors scored it a 3 on the too short (1)/too long (5) scale.

- More than half the visitors think the tour would be improved if information brochures on the collection were available (54 percent). Over one-third like the tour as it is (37 percent); however, this rating varies according to age.

- Almost half the visitors think their visit would have been improved if there were more information on the Russian art collection (45 percent).

Visitors' Self-Rating of Knowledge:

- Visitors think they know the most about "American history" and the least about "Mrs. Post." Generally, visitors' self-rating of knowledge for all subject areas is low; however, some ratings vary according to gender, age, frequency of visits and education level.

Discussion:

This study presents basic demographic information about Hillwood's visitors as well as information regarding visitors' behaviors and experiences. This next section highlights a few findings that deserve special attention from staff. Two topics follow: Audience and Tours.

1) Audience

The demographic profile of visitors indicates which population segments are visiting the Museum and which are not. Such information is useful for museums that want to broaden their audience and develop long-range marketing strategies.

In some ways, Hillwood's visitors are like visitors to many museums. They are highly educated, upper-middle-class and white. However, Hillwood stands alone in two areas: the male/female ratio and age of visitors. Eight out of every ten visitors to Hillwood is female. In addition, the median age is 51.9 years, considerably higher than the mean age of visitors to other museums, which is usually around 38 years. These two demographic characteristics are notable and deserve some discussion.

Much more so than other museum audiences, Hillwood's audience is extremely homogeneous. The nature of the audience may be due to the distinctive nature of the Museum's collection. Hillwood is reaching a very well-defined population. If staff members are interested in increasing their annual attendance, they can easily target and market to that one population. There is a good chance they will be able to recruit new visitors that match their current audience profile, as that population clearly has a strong interest in the Main House and decorative Russian art collection.

If staff members are interested in reaching a more diverse audience, this study can be equally useful in helping the Museum define a target audience. For example, data regarding education could be used as an indicator to target other populations less evident in Hillwood's visitorship that may be interested in visiting Hillwood. Income is less of an indicator because visitors' family income levels are distributed among all income categories. Men generally, younger visitors (under 45 years), and nonwhite visitors are not very visible in Hillwood's audience, yet there are many men (and women) in the Washington, D.C., area alone who are highly educated, young and nonwhite. Marketing efforts could focus on recruiting these local, well-educated nonvisitors. Since more than half of Hillwood's audience is from the Washington, D.C., area (59 percent), and more than three-quarters of those who are local visitors are dedicated repeat visitors (83 percent), Washington, D.C., provides a pool of potential visitors, if not potential dedicated visitors to Hillwood.

This study provides some information about younger visitors. Data show that younger visitors would be more likely to visit on weekend days and evenings, generally, than older visitors. Thus, being open only on Saturdays and on weekdays could be a barrier to recruiting younger audiences. Data also show that younger visitors are more likely to visit the gardens/greenhouse than older visitors, and that the Main House is visited less by younger visitors than older visitors. In addition, more young people visit in July than in October. The gardens can be used as a seasonal marketing tool to attract a younger audience.

Learning more about male, younger female and nonwhite nonvisitors would be advantageous. Focus group discussions can uncover participants' preconceived notions and misconceptions of Hillwood and, ultimately, barriers to visitation. They can also indicate possible directions Hillwood could take to turn nonvisitors into visitors. Alternatively, focus groups with dedicated visitors would also provide useful information. It is useful knowing what visitors find most captivating about a museum—causing them to return, as that information can be used in marketing efforts.

2) Tours

Data generated from the semantic differentials, which isolate and measure fine points of a visitor's experience, present several interesting issues that warrant further discussion. Findings from the whole sample regarding these scales fall into two clear categories: content and comfort level. The two top-ranked scales, boring (1)/interesting (5) and uninformative (1)/informative (5) are both content oriented. Visitors rate them high, as their mean scores are 4.7 and 4.4, respectively.

Praise for the content of the tours surfaces again in responses to the open-ended question at the end of the survey. Most of these comments focus on the knowledge tour guides have of the subject matter. Visitors want information and appreciate that tour guides impart so much to them during their tour. However, findings also show that more than half the visitors want information brochures on the collection, and more than one-third want written descriptions next to the objects. Visitors' high marks for the tours being interesting and informative should not be confused with the idea that some visitors think some types of information are best conveyed through the written word, or that visitors want information in a variety of learning media reflecting varied learning styles.

Three of the scales ask visitors to rate their comfort level: uncomfortable (1)/comfortable (5); overwhelming (1)/manageable (5); and exhausting (1)/relaxing (5). The findings from one scale must always be examined in the context of findings from other scales. These three comfort-level scales did not score as high as the content-oriented scales. In addition, the exhausting (1)/relaxing (5) scale ranked last among the six negative/positive scales. The scale that examined tour length shows that the majority of visitors think the tour length is just right, but this finding must be considered in light of some of the other findings, like the exhausting (1)/relaxing (5) scale. Also, in response to the open-ended question, and without any prompting, 7 percent of visitors say they want more time to browse. They may not want the length of the tour to change, but they may want what happens during the tour to change.

They may also want to feel less exhausted at the end of the tour. So while visitors are satisfied with how much information is being conveyed during a tour, the tour's format is unsatisfactory for some visitors. These findings are reiterated in some of the analysis of variance that were calculated with these data.

With both the content-oriented scales and the three comfort-level scales, there are variations according to day of visit, age and education level.

Weekday visitors rate their overwhelming (1)/manageable (5) and uncomfortable (1)/comfortable (5) experiences higher than do Saturday visitors.

Visitors who are college-educated rate their overwhelming (1)/manageable (5) and uninformative (1)/informative (5) experiences higher than those who are not. Additionally, when only college-educated visitors were isolated and examined regarding day of visit and experience, findings show that even those who are college educated have a more manageable experience on weekdays than on Saturdays. This difference warrants some examination by Hillwood staff.

Regarding age, younger visitors (<54 years) have experiences different from those of older visitors (55+ years). On four of the seven scales, younger visitors rate their experience higher than older visitors. Those scales are: awful (1)/fabulous (5); uncomfortable (1)/comfortable (5); uninformative (1)/informative (5); and overwhelming (1)/manageable (5). This finding is highly unusual, as in general, older visitors, women in particular, rate their experiences higher than younger visitors do. This phenomenon, known as "courtesy bias"[3] must be considered when looking at evaluative findings. So if courtesy bias is factored in, older visitors' (43.4 percent are 55+ years) ratings have to be read as inflated. Thus, the fact that their ratings are lower than younger visitors' ratings is cause for concern—particularly since the majority of Hillwood's visitors are older women. Is Hillwood not meeting the needs of its older visitors, of which there are many? What about the tours makes them more difficult for older visitors? Focus groups or interviews with older visitors could yield valuable information regarding this matter.

Essentially, visitors' experiences on the guided tour vary according to when a visitor visits (a weekday or on Saturday), a visitor's age and a visitor's education level. Not all tour guides are alike—each brings an individual style and skill to his or her work—and not all visitors are alike. What researchers call the visitor experience is the mix of what museum staff offers and what visitors bring with them (who they are [gender, age, etc.], background experiences, learning styles, etc.). To create a successful visitor experience, museum staff must think hard about which aspects of the experience are within their control and which are not. In fact, since it is inappropriate to expect visitors to change who they are, staff must then try to understand visitors for who they are and be flexible in how they teach and work with visitors.

This study did not examine tour experiences from the inside-out (observations during tours were not conducted), so it is impossible to identify aspects of the tour that might account for experiential differences by when the visit takes place, the visitor's age and the visitor's education level. Are groups on Saturdays larger? Are the tours shorter or longer? Do touring techniques differ? Are older visitors treated differently from the way younger visitors are treated? Do tour guides respond differently to visitors who appear to have a more sophisticated knowledge of decorative arts than to those who do not? If there are differences, regardless of whether they are logistical in nature or dependent on the style of any one particular guide, they are worthy of examination.

Visitor Observations on Tour and Interviews after the Tour

Randi Korn & Associates, Inc., in cooperation with the Hillwood Museum, designed a visitor study that focused on observing visitors on tour and interviewing visitors after a tour as part of the Museum's multiyear effort to better understand their visitors' experiences. Members of the Visitor Experience Team (VET) collected nearly all of the data. This team included fifteen dedicated guides who were carefully selected to serve as data collectors and liaisons between the VET team and the other Hillwood guides. VET guides attended monthly meetings where they learned how to collect observations of visitors and conduct face-to-face interviews with visitors. These meetings also provided many opportunities for VET guides to discuss what they were learning from visitors and how studying visitors has helped them be better guides.

The primary objective of this study was to train staff in evaluation methods, to collect visitor feedback about the tour experience and to show guides that understanding visitors' experiences will change the way they think about and do their work.

This segment presents a synopsis of the visitor observation data and visitor interviews. In preparing this document, we searched for meaningful patterns within both data sets. Whether a pattern was meaningful was determined by its frequency or infrequency in the data as well as by its inclusion on the VET Goals document.[4]

All the visitor interviews were tape-recorded, but only 22 were transcribed and analyzed.[5] Interview questions asked visitors about their expectations of the Hillwood Museum, their experiences on tour, how they like to receive information when visiting a museum, and how they think the tour could be improved. At the end of the interview, visitors were asked two additional questions about a specific object (*kovsh*) to understand how they look at and think about works of art.

Hillwood tour guides collected all observation data. The data set comprises 37 observation periods. During each of these observation periods, observers recorded visitors' and guides' behaviors, comments and questions in three or four rooms and during the transition between these rooms. These observation periods took place either at the beginning or at the end of a tour, and, in many cases, observers observed the beginning and end of the same tour. Thus, one tour might be broken into two observation periods.

Observers noted behaviors and comments on a prepared observation data collection sheet. At the end of each observation period, observers were also asked to include any additional comments they thought necessary (e.g., that the group consisted only of family members), as well as the day, time, visitor age range, number of visitors, language skills of group, weather conditions, and whether the group had seen the orientation film.

Summary of Findings and Discussion:

Interviewees spoke about their experiences on tour—focusing on the length of the tour, their feelings of being overwhelmed and the quality of the guides. Comments about tour length and feelings of being overwhelmed were often intertwined, as were comments about tour length and the guide.

The issue of tour length cannot be examined in isolation because it is a complicated issue that is particularly difficult to articulate during a short interview with visitors or by observing them on tour. How much time visitors feel they have to see the house and objects in the rooms is, in part, determined by the number of objects to see. The data clearly show that visitors are overwhelmed by all there is to see in the house. The amount of time visitors feel they have is also dependent upon the guide's behavior as guides lead visitors through the house. If a guide rushes visitors from one room to the next, for example, visitors will feel rushed. Thus, when some visitors say that the tours are too short and there is not enough time to see everything, they might mean, "There is so much to see here, and I feel I need to see as much as I can," or, "I am being moved into another room, and I am not finished looking around this room."

On a more positive note, there is a lot of interaction between the guide and the group and among visitors in the group, as evidenced by the observation data. Visitors were observed chatting appreciatively about the objects, talking about what they were seeing and hearing, and laughing in response to the guide's comments. These findings indicate that, although visitors may want to move at their own pace and may feel rushed at times, overall they are having a positive experience.

Although visitors are provided with an orientation film prior to their tour, perhaps they are not being told enough of the "right" information. While the film shows what some of the rooms look like, the focus is on individual objects—not the overall image of the rooms and all that they hold, which can be visually overwhelming. The interview data suggest that some visitors may need to be prepared for what they are about to experience. Additionally, observation data show that few guides gave introductory remarks (e.g., asking about particular interests) or instructed visitors on the procedures of the tour.

Research on field trips for children shows that when young visitors are prepped before their visit, their on-site experiences are richer and more meaningful. The same likely holds true for adult visitors, although no one has ever studied the effects of previsit strategies on adult museum visitors. Since increasing the length of the tour is not an option at Hillwood, staff must do as much as they can in preparing visitors, in a positive way, for their experience.

The issue of time emerged again when interviewees were asked how their tour could be improved. Many said they want more time to look around, and they did not want to be rushed through the house. In general, interviewees were too focused on the abundance of objects in the house and not focused enough on the meaning of the objects. Furthermore, observation data show that while wandering and lingering to look at objects were prevalent behaviors, suggesting that visitors want to engage in these activities, few guides invited visitors to do so. Visitors need to be prepared for what they will encounter in the house, guides need to be relaxed as they move visitors through the house, and guides must give visitors ample time to study objects of their choosing.

Recommendations:

Prepare visitors for the quantity of objects they will encounter in the house before they enter the house. The orientation film introduces visitors to individual objects but not to the wealth of objects they will see. Tell visitors that there are numerous objects to see in the house, but that it is impossible to see everything in one visit. Additionally, assure them that their guide will do an excellent job of highlighting those objects that best represent the collection. This emphasis in an orientation will likely prepare visitors enough so they can use their energy and time more efficiently and focus on the meaning of objects, rather than the quantity of objects.

Do not rush visitors through the house. Rushing visitors through the house tells visitors that they do not have enough time to see everything. Visitors can sense when a guide is rushing (e.g., continually checking her watch, talking too fast, and telling people to move along quickly). All guides should make decisions about what they want to say to visitors and should convey that information in a relaxed manner—verbally and through body language. If guides are relaxed during the tour, visitors will respond accordingly.

Allow visitors time to look at objects on their own. Reserve a few minutes in each room for silent looking and exploring. Invite curious visitors to ask questions and allow contemplative visitors to study individual objects.

Use focus groups to continue to explore visitors' experiences on tour at Hillwood. Since focus groups allow for lengthy discussions about specific topics, tour length is one issue that can be explored during the focus group discussions.

Interviewees remembered more about Mrs. Post than they did about Russian history, Russian decorative arts or individual objects. Even if visitors did not know about Mrs. Post before their visit, they retained quality information about her. The orientation film likely helps, as does the fact that it is easier to feel a human connection to stories about someone's life than it is about a subject with which one is not familiar, like Russian history or decorative art objects. Some interviewees' remarks also suggest that their lack of knowledge about Russian history was a barrier to their appreciation of the objects. The orientation film also helped some interviewees recognize certain objects, which, coupled with interviewees' ability to remember certain aspects of Mrs. Post's life, show that preparing visitors for what they will see produces positive results. Observation data further support the need for some type of pretour orientation, as the overwhelming majority of visitor questions focused on the objects. If teaching visitors about Russian history and individual objects is important to Hillwood staff, staff will have to provide visitors with a framework for processing information about these subjects.

Recommendations:

Consider redoing the orientation film so it is more effective at introducing visitors to Russian history and decorative arts. Visitors desperately need some grounding in these two areas. Clearly, the orientation film does a good job of introducing visitors to Mrs. Post and some of the objects in the house, but it falls short of providing visitors with information that will help them understand Russian decorative arts and the historical context in which the collection was created.

Offer a range of thematic tours from which visitors can choose when they make their reservation. Allow visitors an option to learn more about Russian history and decorative arts by offering specialized tours. An "Introduction to Russian History" tour, for example, will provide repeat visitors with a new way to experience and view the collection, and it may help first-time visitors feel more comfortable with a new subject. Having a range of tour options available may also encourage repeat visits among visitors.

Hillwood's visitors like to receive information though a range of media. Taking guided tours is preferred by some and others prefer reading.

Recommendation:

> **Offer visitors a range of interpretive media.** Not all visitors are comfortable taking a tour because they prefer to wander around on their own, at their own pace, or they simply prefer to receive information from another medium. Additionally, it is difficult for guides to say all they want to in one tour. Providing visitors with alternative ways to obtain information, and inviting guides to communicate more information through another means, such as labels, information sheets or audio tours, will ultimately provide interested visitors with more information and freedom to choose among interpretive media.

Focus Group Conversations about Hillwood's Tours

Focus groups were conducted to provide staff members with additional information about the visitor experience at Hillwood. The focus groups were also held to better understand visitor experiences on tour—what visitors remember about their tour, what they think the guide was trying to communicate, what kind of information they want to hear when looking at an object and how they perceive Mrs. Post. Staff members were also interested in having focus group participants discuss interpretive methods they like when learning about objects in a museum.

Participants were recruited using a list of 500 names and phone numbers of individuals who had recently visited Hillwood. A screener was used during the initial phone contact to make sure only those who were first-time visitors to Hillwood would be invited to be in the focus groups. Both focus groups were tape-recorded with participants' awareness.

The overarching goal of the focus groups was to obtain feedback about first-time visitors' experiences on tour. Specifically, the goals were to determine:

- visitors' motivation to visit Hillwood;
- visitors' expectations for their visit;
- whether visitors think Hillwood is a historic home or a museum;
- characteristics that constitute an excellent tour;
- characteristics that constitute a poor tour;
- visitors' experiences on tour, including what visitors remember most and what visitors think the guide was communicating;
- visitors' interest in knowing the historical circumstances of objects;
- visitors' perception of Mrs. Post in light of how tour guides and the movie present her;
- the interpretive methods visitors like to use when learning about objects in museums.

Summary of Findings and Discussion:

Participants appeared to be younger than the average age of visitors to Hillwood, as indicated in the 1995 visitor survey. The value of talking with Hillwood's younger visitors is that Hillwood staff desire to attract a younger audience. Thus the discussion that follows will give staff members insight to this new, growing audience.

Similar to the findings of the 1995 visitor survey and the interview and observation data that were collected in 1996, in general visitors are having a positive experience at Hillwood. However, a few issues surfaced in the focus groups that deserve staff attention.

1) Public Understanding of Hillwood

Most participants did not know very much about Hillwood prior to their visit. Participants' reasons for visiting seemed to have more to do with the ambiance and lifestyle that they had heard about than with Hillwood's collection and offerings. Thus, with little or no specific expectations for their visit, participants were generally quite pleased with what they saw and experienced. Most had no idea that the collection is so extensive, and they were overwhelmed and delighted by the quality of their tour and the contents of the house (e.g., knowledgeable guide, friendliness of staff, the way small groups were moved through the house and the fabulous collection of Russian decorative arts).

The discussion about Hillwood's being a historic house or a museum proved interesting. Opinions were mixed, suggesting that Hillwood is not perceived in a clear-cut way. How Hillwood is classified is determined by the visitor and the context in which he or she experiences and sees Hillwood. Those who focus on the house and the gardens think of Hillwood as a historic house, and those who see the collection as the primary feature think of Hillwood as a museum. How a visitor sees an institution is reflective of that individual's perspective, how the institution presents itself to the public and how the media portray the institution. So visitors, the institution and the media shape a visitor's perception of and experience in an institution. From a visitor's point of view, Hillwood can be either a museum, a historic house or both. As noted during one of the discussions, a historic home might appeal to a younger audience, so marketing Hillwood as a historic home might bring in a younger audience. This approach is worth pursuing, as there has been much press lately about the aging arts audience.

While the data show that Hillwood is enjoyed by those who see it as a historic house and those who see it as a museum, staff and board members must delineate the institution's mission and identity. It is worthwhile for staff members to know that the collective experience of Hillwood is not narrow; it can be experienced in multiple ways—depending, among other things, on the visitor's point of view. Programming ideas, including tour offerings, can take advantage of this diversity. Participants realized that there are several ways in which the collection can be presented (e.g., a china tour, an art technique tour, a Russian history tour), suggesting that programming can be diverse to support multiple interests. Through creative public programming, including offering a range of thematic tours, Hillwood will appeal to a new, younger, more diverse audience while continuing to appeal to those who are dedicated Hillwood visitors.

2) The Tour

Similar to interviewees' responses gathered in 1996, when participants talked about their experience on tours, they focused on the issue of time. Time, however, is not a stand-alone issue. That is, how much time one feels is needed relates to the number of objects on display, the way they are displayed and the guide's presentation of the objects, the house and Mrs. Post. While participants were able to speak generically about the objects described to them on tour, few details came through in their recollections. When participants were asked what they thought the guide was communicating, their remarks focused more on Mrs. Post than on the collection or Russian history. As noted earlier, participants did not know very much about Hillwood and they did not have strong expectations for what they would find and experience there. The film provided participants with an excellent overview of Mrs. Post and her life story. The guides, too, according to participants, talked about Mrs. Post and many aspects of her life. It is not unusual that it would be easier for participants to remember details about Mrs. Post than it would be for them to remember information or ideas about objects and Russian history—especially if they had had little or no exposure to Russian decorative arts and Russian history prior to their visit. Additionally, it should be noted that when participants were asked whether they wanted to know more about the historical circumstances surrounding the objects they saw, they expressed little interest. Most felt that the subject of Russian history was too expansive, and knowing the history would not enhance their experience with the objects.

If staff believe that it is important for visitors to take ideas about the objects and Russian history away with them, the film and tour guides will have to present them in a context that will hold meaning for visitors. Additionally, visitors will need to be presented with a conceptual orientation prior to entering the house (films often serve this purpose in museums) because once they enter the house, they are overwhelmed by the objects and environment. After being introduced to some overarching ideas, the content of the tour can accentuate and exemplify those ideas.

Recommendations:

- Appeal to a younger, more diverse audience by marketing Hillwood from multiple perspectives—a historic house, a Russian decorative arts collection, a home of one of America's elite and beautiful gardens.

- Prepare visitors for the environment of the house as part of their orientation so their feeling of being overwhelmed by all that they see becomes less important than the objects in the collection.

- Along with preparing visitors for the environment, also introduce them to the conceptual framework of their tour.

- Provide thematic tours so it is easier for visitors to connect the information imparted by guides with the objects they see.

- Test the appeal and success of these new thematic tours by piloting them and holding focus groups to collect visitor reactions.

- Train guides to ask higher-level thinking questions of visitors, motivating visitors to draw relationships among objects.

- If staff members decide that Russian history is important to teach, strategies for doing so must be carefully conceived and tested as focus group participants expressed little interest in having Russian history be included in their tour. However, studies show that visitors welcome new ideas when they are presented in an accessible way.

ENDNOTES:

1. Hillwood Museum & Gardens' Web site is at www.hillwoodmuseum.org.

2. A guided tour was the only way one could view the collection and house.

3. Courtesy bias is when respondents rate items higher so as not to offend the associated organization.

4. During the first several sessions with the guides, Randi Korn facilitated discussions that focused on writing objectives for the guided tours. These objectives were used as a gauge during analysis.

5. Randi Korn conducted about half of the analyzed interviews. While all 15 guides conducted at least two interviews, some guides were not as skilled at interviewing as others. Therefore, only those interviews that were conducted in an unbiased way were included in the analysis.

Audiences and the Changed Museum

Harold K. Skramstad, Jr., President Emeritus,
Henry Ford Museum & Greenfield Village

As Nancy Bryk and others have noted in their essays, the term "decorative arts" has become an uncomfortable one for many museums. In history museums, the term "decorative arts" reminds us of the degree to which our general vocabulary has evolved from the world of the art museum. But they are the "poor cousins" in art museums with neither the attraction nor the artistic power of great pictures or sculpture. In any case, the term is an increasingly inadequate descriptor for material objects that have a practical function that was often more important to the contemporary user than its artistic or decorative intent. For most history museums the term "decorative arts" seems archaic and in need of replacement. I would suggest that rather than trying to find an all-purpose replacement, each museum develop its own descriptor to meet its own purposes in building a link between these kinds of objects and potential museum audiences.

A number of common threads appear throughout the Symposium papers and suggest some new, exciting and productive strategies for both redefining traditionally shaped "decorative arts" collections and bringing them together in new ways to serve new audiences. Many of the interpretive strategies outlined in the papers will not only help develop new audiences for "decorative arts" collections, but others as well.

Starting with the Audience:

The most striking feature of most of the papers presented at the Symposium is the simple fact that the new exhibition and program strategies described are audience focused. This is worthy of comment in itself. To see in these papers a common strategy that begins program planning with an awareness of audience is heartening. For a number of the organizations represented at the Symposium this is a new strategy; it has taken them into new and probably uncomfortable territory, especially for more traditionally focused and trained curators. Yet it is obvious that those museums willing to take the plunge found that listening to their audiences was a helpful and sometimes even inspiring activity. Museum visitors are in the museum to enjoy and to learn, but not on terms and conditions arbitrarily imposed by the museum. For a number of the museums represented at the Symposium, the project described was their first sustained attempt at a real conversation and dialogue with their audiences. They should be celebrated for it.

Recognition of the Diversity of Audience Expectations:

One of the greatest difficulties in shaping effective museum experiences is addressing the diversity of expectations that museum visitors will bring to the experience. Here is where a number of Symposium participants shared their frustration. We need to acknowledge that well-wrought learning theories are often trumped by visitor reality and that it is probably impossible to develop all-purpose program development theories and strategies that will meet every expectation of every audience. Each museum needs to make some tough choices about which audiences are most important for them to reach in each program or exhibit and set its course accordingly. It was heartening to see so many of the represented museums willing to make clear choices about both audience and content message and shape their communication strategies accordingly.

Audience Research Is Not a Mystery:

I was struck by the fact that staff at so many of the organizations represented at the Symposium participated in simple observation of their visitors as they engaged (or did not engage) with exhibitions, and involved themselves in other simple forms of audience research. While visitor observation and audience research have been around museums for a long time, they too often have been seen as exotic and usually out-sourced skills rather than a continuing core competency of the museum itself. Most successful businesses continue their success by a constant process of observing their customers (and non-customers) and by listening to them. Museums need to embed this same process into everything they do.

Experiment, Experiment, Experiment:

An inevitable consequence of the professionalization of museum practice has been the search for models and "magic bullets" that will provide all-purpose templates for developing powerful learning experiences. The variety of program approaches and outcomes shared at the Symposium is an encouraging statement of how far museums have moved away from this simplistic view of "best professional practices." As each museum becomes less driven by a homogenized body of professional models and more driven by its own distinctive mission and more clearly defined audiences, we will see a richness and variety of practices that will reinforce a sense of institutional distinctiveness and identity for each museum. In the case of the "decorative arts," it would seem that while one museum might appropriately choose to focus on the practical and functional connection of its collection to people's lives, another might use the same kinds of collection materials to help museum learners move from one stage of aesthetic understanding to another.

Rethinking the Production Values of the Exhibit Experience:

Symposium participants paid a great deal of attention to reconceptualizing the learning possibilities of the exhibit experience in terms of audience, theme, experience and content. A consistent lesson shared by most papers was that audiences enjoyed the process of engagement with the museum in shaping the experiences. This would suggest that it might be time to seriously rethink the entire concept of the "exhibition" as a museum production. Traditionally the design and fabrication of exhibits has been seen, and appropriately so, as a special art form as well as a medium of communication. A high premium has traditionally been placed on the fit and finish of the exhibit furniture, the quality of label production, etc. The result has been that exhibits are extremely expensive to design and to fabricate. Once built, the capital investment in changing them is often so great that it precludes the kind of experimentation and change necessary for the museum to be flexible and responsive. Perhaps it is time to rethink the design and production process of exhibits, especially in history museums. I suspect that the present situation is a lot like the design and fabrication of classrooms in elementary schools or corporate research laboratories; their design reflects less the needs of students and researchers and more the values of their designers and producers. While museum practitioners carefully monitor the overall fit and finish of museum exhibition environments, my experience has been that visitors are pretty much oblivious to it.

The immense strides made in electronic technology mean that labels can now be done on flat-screens in a way that allows for almost instant changes in the depth and amount of information and interpretation and even in choice of language. The audio and visual components of exhibitions are now extremely inexpensive technologies and getting more so every day. Exhibit furniture could be designed in a much more provisional way so that it has a useful life measured in months rather than years with great attendant savings.

The outcome of such changes would be the ability to shape, test, reshape, deliver and change visitor experiences with much greater frequency and with much less cost. The result would be experiences that could address a greater variety of audience expectations with a greater variety of content possibilities than is possible doing exhibits the present way.

Change the Process, Change the Museum:

A reoccurring theme in several of the very best papers presented at the Symposium concerns how the changed way of thinking about audiences and collections inevitably brings about organizational pressures that force the museum to begin to rethink the fundamentals of what it does and how it does it. This is an important message, perhaps the most important one to come out of the Symposium. The kind of risk-taking, experimentation and willingness to confront old assumptions and expose them to the requirements of visitor reality that is evidenced in many of these papers is extremely heartening and bodes well for the future of museums.

I would like to end my brief comments with a personal note. The idea of this Symposium was an important one. The honesty and candor that was evidenced in many of the papers will be extremely helpful in a very practical way to future museum planners. A great deal of credit for the success of the Symposium is due its organizers. As someone who has been privileged to work with Donna Braden and Nancy Bryk (although unfortunately not with Gretchen Overhiser) for more than a decade, it has been truly exhilarating to see how their thinking has evolved in such deep, innovative and productive ways over the years—and that the result of this thinking is now taking a variety of public forms. Both the museum field and the public are greatly in their debt.

A Few Steps Forward

Kenneth L. Ames, Chair, Academic Programs
The Bard Graduate Center for Studies in the Decorative Arts

The papers gathered together here provide a range of thoughtful perspectives on the difficulties of presenting museum decorative arts collections to the public. Although a few purport to describe successful ongoing programs, the most illuminating confront varying degrees of failure. What distinguishes these discussions is the candor with which their authors admit to shortcomings in engaging the public at their institutions and the open-mindedness and vigor with which they search for new strategies.

Acknowledging problems can be painful and even professionally risky in institutions. It can be easier and safer to drift along offering the usual fare. But some problems are difficult to ignore. A museum may install its decorative arts collections with fanfare and great expectations only to find that the public stays away in droves. These authors want to know why. What went wrong? Can the situation be corrected?

It would be claiming too much to say that the participants involved in this project came up with thoroughly satisfactory answers to these questions. They did, however, begin to recognize that their problems were not cosmetic but systemic, embedded deep within the concept of decorative arts and within assumptions about those peculiar institutions called museums. The evidence presented here inclines me to believe that finding ways out of the dilemma of widespread public indifference to museum collections will require fundamental changes in the ways museums see themselves, their collections and their relationship to the public.

What might some of these fundamental changes be? To start with, museums might change the way they name and therefore think about the goods they present. That means eliminating the term "decorative arts." When is the last time you heard anyone using that expression in everyday speech? The papers here argue persuasively that "decorative arts" is an alien, stilted term that makes little sense to most people. Discard it in favor of "household furnishings," "household goods," "home furnishings," or something along those lines. Even the humble and unpretentious "antiques" may be a preferable term for old goods.

The term "decorative arts" is unsatisfactory because it is meaningless to the general public and also because it signals "art-think" among the curatorial staff. A major symptom of "art-think" is the delusion that style is the only significant lens through which to view objects. Yet the testimony of these papers is that style—at least as interpreted by decorative arts curators—is something the public simply does not understand or care about. That is in large part because museums exhibit style as an aesthetic abstraction. In fact, most museum visitors are quite knowledgeable about style in their own surroundings, where it operates without being named. They know the difference between a Toyota and a Mercedes, between an S.U.V. and a pickup truck, and they know what those differences imply. They know that style is a dynamic cultural system through which people define themselves and are defined by others. Style is about gender, age, class, ethnicity, education, affluence, region and a host of other things. In real-life situations style rarely bears a label, but people know how to read it nonetheless. When museums slap an aesthetic style term onto an object, they drain the vitality out of it and transform it into a lifeless museum specimen.

A second step in the right direction would be for museum staff to acknowledge the very real limitations under which their institutions operate. Even in the best of circumstances, museums offer only a partial experience, and that may not be enough for many modern visitors. In a plea for promoting public visual literacy, one of the authors here makes a promising but misleading analogy between libraries and museums. Museums are not libraries, not by a long shot. In libraries, people can handle everything. They can take books, tapes and films home with them and own them temporarily. But in most museums people cannot borrow the objects. They are lucky if they can even touch them. The library experience is total, holistic. The museum experience is partial, limited.

Again, what to do? The answer may be twofold. On one hand, museums need to offer visitors as many experiences beyond merely seeing as they possibly can. On the other, they need to make seeing as full an experience as it can possibly be. What complicates the work of museums today is the fact that the world of goods has become highly democratized. Mass production, mass consumption, mass communication and mass education have made goods and knowledge about goods commonplace. In virtually any marketplace today people can have physical, hands-on access to objects of extraordinary variety and quality. But in the museum they still cannot touch. But if we won't let them touch the goods, we have to allow them some sort of compensatory interaction, some opportunity for physical and intellectual engagement with something. The essays here describe several promising alternatives.

If seeing is the most museums can offer, they need to let people really see. They need to acknowledge that *how* something is exhibited can be even more important than *what* is exhibited. My institution recently displayed a world-class exhibition of ancient Roman glass. It was boring beyond belief. Although the installation occupied two floors in the building in which I work, I never bothered to look at the entire exhibition. My fault or that of the exhibition? In a market economy, the customer is always right. In this case, I was the customer and I wasn't buying. The exhibition design made no attempt to engage my late modern visual sense and was very easy to ignore.

If this were a story of one customer lost, it would be insignificant. But I am not alone. There are probably 50 million or more like me who are not going to visit a museum to look at a few dozen little vases and vials lined up in glass cases, ancient Roman or not. Today's visitors are awash in visual and material abundance and simply demand more. The ante is far higher than it used to be.

On a more positive note, some of the papers here indicate that many museum visitors have learned to make the most of seeing. For them, just looking around can be highly satisfying, particularly if there is much to look at and the experience is enhanced in other sensory or affective dimensions. "Just looking around" may strike some museum educators as too lacking in purpose, too undirected to be respectable. If so, that response indicates a need to reconsider what museum learning is all about. Moseying around, to use an old term, seeing what there is to see, is a perfectly satisfactory way of learning. Indeed, looking *is* learning, one of the most fundamental ways that people and other animals learn.

This kind of learning is difficult to control. Don't try. Too narrow an emphasis on teaching facts doesn't work in museums. Museums have to recognize that visitors browse among available offerings, picking up what they want or need at the moment. The meaning visitors make of any exhibition is strongly colored by their own experiences and interests. This truth can be liberating. It means we can give up on the unrewarding business of trying to teach, in the narrow sense of the term, in favor of the far more promising and open-ended strategy of providing visitors with opportunities for learning.

Again, these papers comment usefully on this issue, as they do on many others I cannot discuss here. Two final, inter-related points are worth making, however. The first is that museums will probably succeed best when they treat their visitors with respect and as their peers. It is important to remember that, even though they may not know as much about certain categories of objects as museum staff, every adult museum visitor knows more about *something* than museum staff does. Everyone has a specialty, if only his or her own life. Treating people as intelligent, thinking peers means giving up on telling them what to think. We can tell them what we think and why we think it. We can tell them what we like and why. But they are free to think and to like as they wish. Respect is reciprocated.

My last—and perhaps most contentious observation—is that the split between teaching and providing opportunities for learning, between telling people what to think and honoring their values and interpretations, breaks down along art and history lines. Overstating a bit, the art museum folk want to teach, while the history museum folk want to provide opportunities for learning. To my mind, the history folks have seen the light but the art folks dwell in darkness still. The difference may derive from the specifics of these two different orientations to the material world. In the last half century, history has been democratized but no such reformation has swept over the art world, which remains its old hierarchical, anti-democratic and dogmatic self.

I encourage readers to sort through the historians and the art folk here and decide for themselves if this interpretation holds water. If so, my final prescription for change is to democratize the concept of art or, if that is too great a task, throw it out altogether. The reigning concept is exclusivist, elitist and socially and economically dysfunctional. The art world is still dominated by the sense of superiority and condescension toward the public that got decorative arts installations into dire predicaments in the first place. Although no one uses the tired old expression "art appreciation" anymore, art museums are still trying to tell people what to like and what to think. Museums of all stripes should stop teaching and stop preaching. Let the people look around and learn for themselves. And if they seem to be having a good time, you're probably doing something right.

Who Dusts All This?

Beverly Serrell, Director, Serrell & Associates

Room after room of chairs, tables, rugs, things on the walls—Who does dust all this stuff, anyway? That is a practical, concrete question straight from the heart of a visitor's experience. As the papers in this volume testify, listening to your visitors doesn't always mean you will like what you hear.

Are visitor studies in decorative arts institutions and exhibitions any different from visitor studies in other places? They are, but only by degree. Audience surveys have shown that the decorative arts attract a higher percentage of female and older visitors compared to other museum topics (Korn), and the guided-tour method of interpretation is used more often—sometimes exclusively—compared with other collections. There are, on the other hand, strong similarities with the non-decorative arts as well: Many people are making their first visit and they are coming as a social group, spending a short time and attending for many of the same reasons. Many museum visitors are "Stage I" learners, regardless of the topic, although the decorative arts are probably unusual in that most visitors can't even define the term (Dietz, Brotman and Wintemberg) and have huge difficulties with the vocabulary of style, e.g., Baroque, Rococo, Gothic (Durbin).

Reaching Out:

Like many other museums, the ones represented in this Symposium are reaching out to new audiences through diversified marketing efforts, reinterpreted collections and innovative programming. These efforts make the issue of vocabulary even more important. To call it "home furnishings on a big budget" is a big step in the direction of making the decorative arts more accessible. The other changes, such as adding hands-on activities in galleries (Disviscour and Jones), having guides carry visual aids to supplement the tours (Carlisle), writing labels with dramatic dialogue (Dietz, Brotman and Wintemberg), and using questioning strategies that are based on the visitors' experience (Trager) or exploring the visitors' role as expert (Durbin) all sound like wonderful ideas to me.

Reaching new audiences, as many Symposium papers point out, has to be instigated initially on the audience's diverse terms. What educational theories inform our efforts? What is "education" in a museum setting? What constitutes a "theory"? We toss these terms around assuming that others know what we mean, but much of visitor studies research is more practical and empirical than theoretical. Compared to educational programming in schools, museum exhibits that are randomly accessed and seen for brief episodes are difficult laboratories in which to study learning or learners—especially learners who don't even call themselves that. Housen's theory is useful for fine arts education, but it doesn't seem to translate that easily into a theory that guides practice in a decorative arts exhibition (Yenawine). Yet parts of her theory can provide helpful insights for developing open-ended interactions between staff and visitors (Podos), a very good way to reach visitors on their own level.

Reading about these many good ideas inspired me to come up with a little questioning strategy of my own. Saul Bass, a designer in the 1960s, said, "Design is thinking made visual." It seems that we could ask of the decorative arts, "What were they thinking (when they made this)?" and "Who were they?" Regardless of age, gender, socioeconomic status, etc., visitors' own experiences with home furnishings can be called upon for many meaningful answers. (The next question is, can we leave it at that, or do we have to fall back into providing "historical reality" in the mode of museum-as-expert?)

What About Evaluation?

What about more summative evaluations that show evidence of success and demonstrate the effectiveness of these new techniques in reaching new audiences? These papers offered examples of ways in which evaluations were used to test visitors' prior knowledge, survey their demographic characteristics and to let people try out a prototype. But convincing, systematic summative evaluations were mostly missing. Even the largest study had sample sizes so small that the authors interpreted the results with caution (Disviscour and Jones). This is not a unique situation in the decorative arts; summative studies are not done in the majority of museums. Anecdotal evidence and "unscientific" surveys are still the most common ways of documenting impact (Carlisle), and success is often equated with popularity and selling out (Trager, Podos)—or by a lack of complaints (Dietz, Brotman and Wintemberg).

Interviewing and observing visitors can be exciting and informative, and, as Symposium participants noted, telling (Durbin) and humbling (Disviscour and Jones). Realistic views of what visitors know, do and say about your exhibits and programs must become indispensable in the evaluation process if you are truly dedicated to a visitor-centered approach.

In several cases, however, there was a tendency to dismiss expectations of learning or accountability for it, because of the belief that visitors come for a leisure activity, not to learn facts, recall themes or recognize concept groupings. This is a cop-out. In my experience, in all types of exhibitions, when exhibit teams can clearly articulate their communication goals and use appropriate measurement techniques, they can skillfully document the degree to which they were successful in achieving their objectives. Intent of the museum developers must be matched with evidence of visitor outcomes or impacts. Did you accomplish what you set out to do? Try using the technique of asking learning questions of visitors who have been recruited (with a small reward) to participate in your evaluation studies—visitors who agree to pay more attention. This strategy shifts the question to whether we communicate successfully with visitors who are motivated to learn. If these people can't decipher your conceptual thematic organization or recall personally meaningful ideas, there's little hope that you are communicating well with other visitors!

Beyond the Tour:

In the quest for a visitor-centered approach, there are many stumbling blocks along the trail—philosophical, economical and logistical problems. The one that seems to me to be most problematic to the decorative arts is the logistic of touring visitors in groups. Being herded through limited-access rooms—no touching allowed—with a bunch of strangers is not my idea of a free-ranging, social museum encounter with objects and interactive devices and no time limit. No matter how well trained, articulate or poised the docent is, it's not my favorite mode of museum learning. Visitors (like me) need more variety in the types of interpretation, better orientation up front (why did Mrs. Post like Russian stuff?), and, hopefully, some chance to wander on their own (Korn), even if that means installing expensive security systems to take the place of a guide or guard. If the decorative arts are going to attract more diverse audiences, they need to be interpreted in more diverse, practical, imaginative and meaningful ways. Will you really answer the question, "Who dusts all this?"

The paper that impressed me the most was "Making a New Home for the Decorative Arts in Newark" (Dietz, Brotman and Wintemberg) because the authors went the farthest to specify exactly who they wanted to reach in a new audience; they consciously gave up the most traditional approaches; and they tried the riskiest variety of creative new ways to share the multiple meanings of their home furnishings. I wish that the Lila Wallace Readers' Digest Fund could now come up with the cash for a thorough summative evaluation to find out if the new audiences can see, hear, read and understand themselves better in the new exhibits.

Keep Learning:

Visitor studies, as a body of knowledge, are a century old and still growing vigorously. Symposium participants cited many important studies that inform our practices today, and I would like to offer three more good references: (1) The Museum Learning Collaborative (MLC), a five-year project funded by several government agencies, is studying learning in museums from a theoretical basis. Their Web site (www.mlc.lrdc.pitt.edu/mlc/) has an excellent, extensive annotated bibliography, and they are well into the research phase of their studies. (2) *Insights: Museums, Visitors, Attitudes, and Expectations* is a ten-year-old publication of the Getty Center for Education resulting from a project that involved 11 art museums and numerous visitors in focus groups. It's out of print now, but look for a copy in the libraries of art museums in Boston, Brooklyn, Chicago, Cleveland, Dallas, Denver, Los Angeles, D.C., Toledo and Seattle. (3) *Curator*, Volume 42, Number 2, April 1999, contains several reports of studies conducted at the Smithsonian in recent years and an excellent bibliography organized by different topics of visitor studies. If there is one piece of advice I have for museum practitioners, it's to read more.

Adopting a new approach was clearly a growing experience for the staffs of the Symposium participants. Making that growth stick—that is, become institutionalized and not disappear when a certain team disbands or a staff member takes another job—is another story. Professional development is crucial to institutionalizing visitor studies. The more staff involved in visitor studies research, the better, especially when they cut across traditional job territories to mix curatorial, educational and design tasks. Developing and implementing visitor studies yourself is certainly possible (Twiss-Garrity), but getting a jump-start by an outside evaluator who is brought in specifically to train in-house staff (Korn) is a good way to avoid reinventing the wheel. I certainly hope that the benefits gained from the new approaches discussed here are lasting ones.